INTRODUCTION TO

WRITTEN LEGAL SKILLS

FOR SQE2

Bethany Brown

Series editors: Amy and David Sixsmith

First published in 2025 by Fink Publishing Ltd

Impression number 10 9 8 7 6 5 4

British Library Cataloguing in Publication Data
A catalogue record for this book is available from the British Library.
ISBN: 9781917183130

This book is also available in various ebook formats.
Ebook ISBN: 9781917183147

Cover and text design by BMLD (bmld.uk)
Production and typesetting by Westchester Publishing Services UK
Development editing by Llinos Edwards

Fink Publishing Ltd
E-mail: hello@revise4law.co.uk
www.revise4law.co.uk

Acknowledgements

The author and publisher would like to thank the following copyright holder for their kind permission to use material in this book:
RELX (UK) Limited, trading as LexisNexis: *Halsbury's Laws of England*, pp. 50, 77 and 79.
The Solicitors Regulation Authority, pp. 52, 54 and 148.
Extracts from the SRA website in this book are owned by and published under licence from the Solicitors Regulation Authority of The Cube, 199 Wharfside Street, Birmingham, B1 1RN, which asserts its right to be identified as the author of this work in accordance with the Copyright, Designs and Patents Act 1988 Sections 77 and 78: www.sra.org.uk/solicitors/standards-regulations/financial-services-conduct-business-rules/. Please refer to the SRA website to ensure you are relying upon the correct version and most up to date version of the Standards.
Every effort has been made to obtain necessary permission with reference to copyright material. The publishers apologise if inadvertently any sources remain unacknowledged and will gladly make suitable arrangements with any copyright holders whom it has not been possible to contact.

Notes from the publisher

1. While Fink Publishing has made every attempt to ensure that advice on the qualification and its assessment is accurate, the official specification and associated assessment guidance materials are the only authoritative source of information and should always be referred to for definitive guidance. See the SRA website at https://sqe.sra.org.uk. Note that the SRA may amend their assessment guidance (including the contents of the assessment specifications) at any point.
2. Fink Publishing has robust editorial processes to ensure the accuracy of the content in this publication, and every effort is made to ensure this publication is free of errors. We are, however, only human, and occasionally errors do occur. Fink Publishing is not liable for any misunderstandings that arise as a result of errors in this publication, but it is our priority to ensure that the content is accurate. If you spot an error, please do contact us at **revise4law.co.uk** so we can make sure it is corrected.

Contents

Contributors

THE AUTHOR

Bethany Brown is a senior lecturer in law at Nottingham Trent University. Previously an assistant solicitor at a high-street law firm, she is now a non-practising solicitor and a fellow of Advance HE. She also has a Postgraduate Certificate in Learning and Teaching in Higher Education. Bethany has taught family law, applied legal knowledge and land law to undergraduates. She has also taught criminal litigation, property practice, legal skills, family law and medical ethics at postgraduate level. Bethany is involved with the teaching and development of the SQE content on the SQE2 Preparation course.

SERIES EDITORS

Dr Amy Sixsmith is associate professor in law at the University of Sunderland and a senior fellow of Advance HE.

Dr David Sixsmith is assistant professor at Northumbria Law School and a senior fellow of Advance HE.

Introduction

Welcome to *Revise SQE: Legal Skills for SQE2*! This series of revision guides is designed to support you through the second element of your Solicitors Qualifying Examination, in which you will be tested on your ability to put the legal knowledge you acquired for your SQE1 assessment into six different practical contexts.

This SQE2 revision guide offers a comprehensive overview of the written skills in the context of professional conduct issues that may arise in your assessment and in practice. It systematically breaks down the Solicitors Regulation Authority's (SRA's) assessment criteria for all written skills, explaining what the SRA considers to be competent or not competent in their performance indicators (PIs). Furthermore, it focuses on how to identify ethical and professional conduct issues and exercise your judgement to resolve them honestly and with integrity, by outlining the SRA Principles, the SRA's Code of Conduct for Solicitors, RELs and RFLs (registered European lawyers and registered foreign lawyers, respectively), and guidance from the SRA and Practice Directions. The guide provides a step-by-step approach to these skills, along with 'Have a go' sections where you can practise your skills in digestible stages. There is also strategic advice to help you prepare effectively for the SQE2 assessments.

The key to successfully navigating your SQE2 assessment can be split into three distinct areas:
- understanding how you are being assessed and what you are being assessed on
- practising example scenarios
- comparing and contrasting your answers with sample answers.

Our SQE2 guides are here to help you with this process, providing you not only with helpful guidance and top tips for approaching all of the relevant skills, but also with sample questions for each assessable skill in each of the relevant legal disciplines. Samples of high- and lower-scoring threshold answers to each question are provided to guide you in good practice – and steer you away from potential pitfalls.

Using this series in conjunction with our series of SQE1 revision guides, to ensure that your legal knowledge is accurate and up to date, will enable you to tackle your SQE2 assessment with confidence.

PREPARING YOURSELF FOR SQE

The SQE is the route to qualification for aspiring solicitors and consists of two parts, as shown in this table.

Assessment	Contents of assessment
SQE1	• 360 multiple-choice questions • Closed book • Assessed over 2 sittings • Over 10 hours in total
SQE2	• Practical legal skills • 16 written and oral assessments • Assesses 6 practical legal skills • Over 14 hours in total

In addition to the above assessments, all candidates will have to undertake two years' qualifying work experience. More information on the SQE assessments can be found on the SRA website.

It is important to note that the SQE can be perceived to be a 'harder' set of assessments than the Legal Practice Course (LPC). The reason for this, explained by the SRA, is that the LPC is designed to prepare candidates for 'day one' of their training contract; the SQE, on the other hand, is designed to prepare candidates for 'day one' of being a newly qualified solicitor. With that in mind, and a different style of assessments in place, it is understandable that you might feel nervous or wary of the SQE.

This revision guide series will focus on preparation for SQE2. The SQE2 assessment is challenging as it asks candidates to put into practice the knowledge that they acquired for SQE1. This style of assessment is likely to be different from what you will have experienced before. In this Introduction and revision guide series, we hope to alleviate some of those concerns, with guidance on preparing for the SQE assessment, tips on how to approach the skills-based assessments and detailed commentaries on sample answers to aid your revision.

WHAT DOES SQE2 ENTAIL?

SQE2 is split into two parts: oral and written. The table below shows the contexts in which these skills are assessed.

Part	Skills	Contexts
Oral	Client interview and attendance note/legal analysis (hereafter referred to as 'interviewing')	Property practice Wills and intestacy, probate administration and practice
	Advocacy	Dispute resolution Criminal litigation
Written	Case and matter analysis Legal research Legal writing Legal drafting	Criminal litigation Dispute resolution Property practice Wills and intestacy, probate administration and practice Business organisations, rules and procedures

ORAL SKILLS

You will sit four oral skills examinations, which will take place over two half-days.

On day one you will be assessed in:
- advocacy in the context of dispute resolution
- interviewing in the context of property practice.

On day two you will be assessed in:
- advocacy in the context of criminal litigation
- interviewing in the context of wills and intestacy, probate administration and practice.

WRITTEN SKILLS

For the written skills assessment, you will sit twelve examinations that will take place over three half-days. Every day you will be required to take an assessment in *each* of the written skills – legal research, case and matter analysis, legal writing and legal drafting.

On day one you will sit:
- two assessments in dispute resolution
- two assessments in criminal litigation.

On day two you will sit:
- two assessments in property practice
- two assessments in wills and intestacy, probate administration and practice.

On day three you will sit all four assessments in business organisations, rules and procedures.

HOW IS SQE2 MARKED?

Each of the SQE2 skills has its own set of assessment criteria. The *Revise SQE: Legal Skills for SQE2* series will include the following:
- Oral skills – the criteria are outlined in the introductory chapters of **Oral Skills for SQE2: Client Interviewing and Negotiation** and **Oral Skills for SQE2: Advocacy**.
- Written skills – the criteria are outlined at the beginning of each chapter in our books covering the written skills for different legal contexts (see pages 3, 34, 88 and 119 in this text).

The assessment is marked against the relevant criteria using the following scale:
A. Superior performance: well above the competency requirements of the assessment.
B. Clearly satisfactory: clearly meets the competency requirements of the assessment.
C. Marginal pass: on balance, just meets the competency requirements of the assessment.
D. Marginal fail: on balance, just fails to meet the competency requirements of the assessment.
E. Clearly unsatisfactory: clearly does not meet the competency requirements of the assessment.
F. Poor performance: well below the competency requirements of the assessment.

Your mark will be calculated by converting the grade into a numerical mark, with A representing 5 marks and F representing 0 marks.

The scaled scoring system

In January 2025 the SRA introduced a scaled scoring system for all SQE2 assessments. This approach is designed to ensure that candidate scores are comparable across different assessment sittings, thereby providing a fair and consistent measure of candidate performance. The same system has already been implemented for all SQE1 assessments.

The scaled scoring system works in the following way:
- Initially, candidates will receive a 'raw score' based on their performance across the 16 assessment stations in SQE2.
- A pass mark is then set for each assessment window. The pass mark is determined using statistical methods that account for any differences in question difficulty. This ensures fairness across different exam versions.
- Candidate raw scores are then converted to a common scale ranging from 0 to 500, with the pass mark consistently set at 300. This standardisation allows for direct comparisons between candidates' performances, regardless of the specific assessments they completed.

When you access your results, you will be able to see:
- a detailed breakdown of your results by assessment station (results will be expressed as marks from 0 to 5 for each assessment criterion across each of the 16 assessment stations)
- your overall mark expressed as a percentage
- your scaled score out of 500 – remember that the pass mark will always be set at 300.

For more information about the scaled scoring system, visit the SRA website.

It is very important that you are aware of the standard you are required to meet. The competence standard is that of a Day One Solicitor, which is mapped against Level 3 of the Threshold Standard for the Statement of Solicitor Competence. This is available on the SRA website, and we would encourage you to review this prior to sitting your SQE2 assessment.

The assessors

In terms of who will be assessing you against this standard and the relevant skills criteria, the interview will be marked by the person you are interviewing, while the remaining assessments (attendance note, advocacy and all written skills) will be marked by a solicitor. All assessors will have received training on how to assess a candidate's performance against the relevant criteria. It is therefore essential that you tackle your assessments in the same way that you would if you were a fully qualified solicitor on the first day of practice – with professionalism, confidence and calmness. This will come across to the assessors in the examination itself: remember that they are fundamentally assessing your suitability for practice!

WHERE DOES *REVISE SQE* COME INTO IT?

This new series of revision guides for SQE2 will provide you with helpful tips and advice on how to tackle each skills assessment in the relevant contexts. Each book provides a range of example threshold answers to SQE2-style assessment questions, which you can use to practise and assess your answers against, to see how you are performing in each individual area. This is designed to assist with your revision and consolidate your understanding of how key topics could be assessed in the SQE2 examination. We hope that this series will give clarity for the assessment focus, provide useful tips for sitting SQE2 and also act as a general revision aid.

Finally, always keep in mind that while SQE2 is primarily a skills-based assessment, you are still being tested on your knowledge of the law. It is therefore important that you conduct an honest self-evaluation on the areas of the SQE1 specification with which you feel you need further support. *Revise SQE* can help you with this:

- Review the 'SQE1 Revision Checklist' for each of our SQE1 revision guides on our website: **www.revise4law.co.uk**. These will help you to identify which substantive topics you feel confident about being assessed on, and which ones you need to revise.
- All of our *Revise SQE* revision guides are mapped to the relevant SRA specifications. Before taking the SQE2 assessments, remember to look back at our revision guides for SQE1 if you have any gaps in your legal knowledge.

Case and matter analysis

■ INTRODUCTION TO CASE AND MATTER ANALYSIS

This chapter explores the written legal skill of case and matter analysis: what it is, why it is an important legal skill for a solicitor, how it relates to the other written legal skills you will be learning, and how case and matter analysis is assessed for SQE2. This includes an outline of the SRA's threshold for a competent Day One Solicitor.

Next, the chapter will consider the criteria against which you will be assessed in the case and matter analysis SQE2 assessment, with a detailed commentary of each point.

Finally, this chapter will demonstrate a stepped approach to case and matter analysis in the context of a contentious dispute resolution case study (question 1). We have provided two sample answers for you to scrutinise. Thereafter you will have the opportunity to practise your own case and matter analysis skills in response to a business practice scenario in question 2, and produce a response. Again, there will be two sample answers which you can use to help you reflect on your own answer.

WHAT IS CASE AND MATTER ANALYSIS, AND WHY IS IT AN IMPORTANT SKILL FOR A SOLICITOR?

Case and matter analysis is a vital skill in practice, and is not to be underestimated. It is the ability to apply relevant legal tests/principles/reasoning to a client's case in order to provide them with advice on their legal position. Whilst that may sound simple, much like the law, the process of case and matter analysis is not often so clean cut. In practice, a client does not always volunteer the required facts and will often provide you with irrelevant information. This means that case and matter analysis is an ongoing skill which you exercise throughout a case, and not just at the beginning. You need to weigh up the strengths and weaknesses of your client's case to ensure that you are giving appropriate advice.

Although case and matter analysis is a legal skill which is assessed on a standalone basis by the SRA, this does not mean it cannot be utilised for your other SQE2 assessments. Far from it: case and matter analysis is a fluid skill relevant to all areas of learning for SQE2, and you will be able to apply the knowledge you attain from this chapter for your other SQE2 assessments. Table 1.1 shows how the other SQE2 assessments link to case and matter analysis.

HOW IS CASE AND MATTER ANALYSIS ASSESSED IN SQE2?

The SQE2 written centralised assessments take place over three half-days. You will be assessed on your case and matter analysis skills on each day:
- Day one – in the context of dispute resolution or criminal litigation.
- Day two – in the context of property practice or wills and intestacy, probate administration and practice.
- Day three – in the context of business organisations, rules and procedures.

Table 1.1 Examples of how case and matter analysis skills can be applied to other SQE2 assessments

Skills	Relevance of case and matter analysis to the skill
ORAL SKILLS	
Client interviewing and negotiation	An assessment might ask you to advise a property client about a dispute with a neighbour. The SQE2 assessment criteria require you to ask effective questions. You would need to complete a case analysis to establish what information you need to find out, to decide whether or not the client's case meets the relevant legal elements.
Attendance note/legal analysis	Following the client interview, you will be asked to complete an attendance note. The SQE2 assessment criteria require you to demonstrate a client-focused approach. You would need to complete a matter analysis to establish the relevant options and specific advantages and disadvantages from the client's perspective. For example, if the property client is aspiring to maintain a friendly relationship with the neighbour, pursuing court action may not be in the client's best interests, even if it is one of the relevant options.
Advocacy	You might be asked to represent the Crown Prosecution Service at a sentencing hearing. To address the SQE2 assessment criteria, you would need to apply the sentencing guidelines to the facts of the case. You would need to complete a case and matter analysis during your preparation, first to establish the relevant aggravating and mitigating facts, and then to apply those to the sentencing guidelines in order to advocate for a suitable sentence.
WRITTEN SKILLS	
Legal research	An assessment might require you to complete some research in relation to a business matter. Part of the requirement is that you have to produce a written note explaining your legal reasoning and the key sources that you are relying on, as well as the advice that should be given to the client. You would need to complete a case and matter analysis to ensure that your research is relevant to the client's circumstances, and that, based on your analysis, your advice is carefully reasoned.
Legal writing	In an assessment you might be asked to write a letter of advice to a client regarding a contentious dispute resolution matter. The assessment criteria require you to include relevant facts, provide client-focused advice, identify ethical and professional conduct issues and exercise judgement to resolve them honestly and with integrity. You would need to complete a case analysis to establish the relevant facts, and a matter analysis to discover whether any professional conduct issues impact your ability to progress the client's case.
Legal drafting	An assessment might ask you to vary an existing will and draft some amendments. You would need to complete a case and matter analysis to ensure that what you draft meets the client's objectives, and that the will is concise and legally comprehensive.

For the case and matter analysis standalone assessment you will complete a 60-minute computer-based assessment. You will be required to produce a written report for a partner which provides a legal analysis of the case and client-focused advice. The assessment will comprise a case study and relevant documents that you will be required to analyse for the basis of your report. You might be asked to include different options and/or suggested approaches to negotiation.

To pass the SQE2 assessment, you must demonstrate that you can meet the SRA's standard of competency of a Day One Solicitor in all four written skills and both oral skills: see Table 1.2.

It is crucial that you are able to identify key facts and analyse the strengths and weakness of a case, in order to provide accurate, high-quality legal advice.

Table 1.2 What is the SRA's threshold for a competent Day One Solicitor?

No.	Skills for an SRA-competent Day One Solicitor
1	Draw on functioning legal knowledge (FLK). Whilst SQE2 is skills-focused, the SRA still expects a Day One Solicitor to be able to identify and apply applicable legal principles in a skills context.
2	Demonstrate an acceptable standard of work. What is deemed acceptable depends on how routine or complex the task may be.
3	Show that you can exercise autonomy to progress matters, whilst being able to recognise when you need support from a colleague.
4	Be able to deal with straightforward transactions and the occasional complex matter.
5	Demonstrate an understanding of the client's perspective, and use this as your focus when establishing the strategy for the case.
6	Be able to check information provided and form judgements about possible courses of action.

Whilst you may have some experience in completing case and matter analysis, either in practice or during undergraduate study, this does not necessarily mean you will meet the criteria set by the SRA. It is essential for you to focus your revision on the SRA's expectations of a Day One Solicitor.

SRA Principles

You will need to bear in mind the SRA Principles, which include the fundamental principles of ethical behaviour that the SRA expects you to uphold. These principles are very important as they safeguard the wider public interest and the integrity of the legal profession.

The SRA Principles are as follows:

As a solicitor, REL or RFL, you must act:
1. in a way that upholds the constitutional principle of the rule of law, and the proper administration of justice.
2. in a way that upholds public trust and confidence in the solicitors' profession and in legal services provided by authorised persons.
3. with independence.
4. with honesty.
5. with integrity.
6. in a way that encourages equality, diversity and inclusion.
7. in the best interests of each client.

■ ASSESSMENT CRITERIA AND COMMENTARY

As you prepare your answer in the SQE2 assessment for case and matter analysis, remember that it will be judged against the following criteria:

SQE2 case and matter analysis assessment criteria

Skills assessment criteria
1. Identify relevant facts.
2. Provide client-focused advice (ie advice which demonstrates an understanding of the problem from the client's point of view and what the client wants to achieve, not just from a legal perspective).
3. Use clear, precise, concise and acceptable language.

Application of law assessment criteria

4. Apply the law correctly to the client's situation.
5. Apply the law comprehensively to the client's situation, identifying any ethical and professional conduct issues and exercising judgement to resolve them honestly and with integrity.

Let us look more closely at each point in these criteria, and explore the SRA's standard of competency as detailed in their performance indicators for SQE2 case and matter analysis.

SKILLS ASSESSMENT CRITERIA

1. Identify relevant facts

Whilst this may seem obvious, it is often difficult to select only the facts that are relevant and discount other, irrelevant information.

You will demonstrate **competence** if you are able to select facts that are important for meeting the client's needs and/or objectives.

You will **not** demonstrate **competence** if you:
- are not selective and instead refer to all the facts
- refer only to irrelevant facts
- do not refer to enough relevant facts to support the legal analysis.

Assessment technique

When eliciting relevant facts during the assessment, you can save time by using the computer's copy and paste function. The SRA has provided guidance that the copy and paste function for the actual SQE2 written assessment is slightly different from the functionality in the Pearson VUE test platform. Make sure you use CTRL+C on your keyboard to copy text and CTRL+V to paste.

2. Provide client-focused advice

Provide advice that demonstrates an understanding of the problem from the client's perspective and what the client wants to achieve, not just from a legal perspective. When advising a client, it is important to think outside the box. You may feel that if a client's case meets the relevant legal elements, they should proceed with court action. However, just because a client can pursue court action does not mean it is always in their best interests. Keep in mind the SRA's Principle 7 that you must act in your client's best interests. You need to focus on the client's goal and their circumstances. Court action is often a lengthy, costly and stressful process for a client, and it might not be in a client's best interest if their goal is not financial compensation.

You will demonstrate **competence** if you can:
- demonstrate an understanding of the client's problem from their perspective
- address any relevant commercial considerations and/or the client's personal circumstances, priorities, objectives and constraints.

You will **not** demonstrate **competence** if you:
- do not approach or appreciate the client's problem from the client's perspective
- do not focus on the issues identified by the client.

3. Use clear, precise, concise and acceptable language

It is crucial to use appropriate language in your SQE2 assessment. Let's break down what the above terms mean for developing your writing skills.
- **Clear:** your work needs to be easy to understand and read.
- **Precise:** your work should contain exact and accurate information, which you can demonstrate by selecting only the relevant facts for a case and matter analysis.
- **Concise:** your response needs to be short and clear, expressing what needs to be said without including unnecessary words. Remember you have limited time in the assessments, so it is essential to be concise.
- **Acceptable:** avoid using unnecessary legal terms that are not appropriate and/or may cause confusion for the reader.

Assessment technique

The SRA has provided guidance that the reader of your case and matter analysis will be a partner in a firm. However, make sure you read the instructions carefully, as the question might state that the partner will use your analysis as a basis for a letter to send to the client. In this case, you should ensure that you use clear, precise, concise and acceptable language which is suitable for *both* the partner and client.

You will demonstrate **competence** if you:
- use understandable language which has a clarity of expression, basing your choice of words on the identity of the reader
- avoid using unnecessary technical terms and legal jargon.

You will **not** demonstrate **competence** if:
- the reader would struggle to understand your use of language, which can occur if your answer lacks clarity or is poorly expressed
- the reader's understanding is adversely affected by the density, length or brevity of the answer.

Assessment technique: spelling and grammatical errors

Remember that there is no spellcheck or highlighting function in the SQE2 written assessment. But do not worry: you will not lose marks for spelling mistakes or grammatical errors that do not impact the legal accuracy, clarity and/or certainty of the written text, or which would ordinarily be flagged by spellcheck functionality. Follow these tips to avoid losing marks:
- Check the spelling of names, addresses, dates and values, as spellcheck would not always pick up on these errors.
- Try to avoid making grammatical errors that might impact the validity of the advice, such as using the passive tense rather than active tense. For example:
  - 'The claimant is requesting damages' is active tense.
  - 'Damages are requested by the claimant' is passive tense.
  The two are not interchangeable, and your advice to the client might differ, depending on whether damages are to be requested or they have already been requested.
- Review your answer to ensure that the tense you are writing in is consistent with the facts.
- Make sure that your work is accessible to the reader.

APPLICATION OF LAW ASSESSMENT CRITERIA

4. Apply the law correctly to the client's situation

You must not neglect your FLK when revising SQE2. The assessments for SQE2 incorporate the legal principles you will have learned for your SQE1 examinations. If there are any gaps in your knowledge, we recommend you familiarise yourself with the contents of the *Revise SQE* revision guides covering SQE1 topics: details of all titles are available at **revise4law.co.uk.**

> ### Assessment technique
>
> You will not be expected to know or address a level of legal detail that a Day One Solicitor would need to look up, such as referencing specific legislation or case law. You would only be expected to know this if you have been provided with materials that contain the answer.
>
> For example, in a property law context, if you are provided with official copies and told to advise on restrictions, it would be reasonable to expect you to identify whether there is a restrictive covenant and explain whether it is legally binding. Your key focus should be to evidence that you have sufficient legal knowledge, which makes you competent to practise on the basis that you can look up further detail at a later stage.

You will demonstrate **competence** if you can identify the relevant fundamental legal principles and apply them correctly.

You will **not** demonstrate **competence** if you:
- do not identify the relevant legal principles
- do not correctly apply those legal principles to the client's case in a way that addresses their needs and concerns.

5. Apply the law comprehensively to the client's situation

You need to identify any ethical and professional conduct issues and exercise judgement to resolve them honestly and with integrity.

Let's look closer at the wording of this assessment criterion.

'Comprehensively'
In the assessment, the legal issues may or may not be explicit.
- If they are not explicit, you might be awarded marks under the comprehensive element if you can successfully identify the legal issues.
- If the legal issues are made explicit, marks for legally comprehensive might be awarded for giving a thorough analysis of those issues, not only for identifying them.

'Ethical and professional conduct issues'
This is a clear statement that professional conduct and ethics are core parts of the SQE2 assessment. However, these conduct and ethical issues will not be necessarily flagged up in the question, and the onus is on you to exercise your professional judgement to identify and resolve any ethical and professional conduct issue with honesty and integrity, as per SRA Principles 4 and 5.

For example:
- **Ethical issues**: a solicitor should consider their client's time and financial resources. It would be unethical to agree to an unattainable deadline or pursue an unwinnable case which drains the client's funds.
- **Professional conduct issues**: where the client is a company, a solicitor should consider the interests of additional parties. In such circumstances, you need to ensure that you have the consent of all parties before you take instructions from one individual. This might take the form of authorisation by board minutes.

You will demonstrate **competence** under these circumstances:
* Your legal analysis is 'sufficiently detailed' in the context of the client's case. To achieve this, you need to demonstrate that you are evaluating relevant information to identify key issues and risks, and can reach reasonable conclusions which are supported by appropriate evidence.
* You refer to pertinent ethical issues and/or the SRA Principles and rules of professional conduct.

You will **not** demonstrate **competence** under these circumstances:
* Your analysis is not 'sufficiently detailed' – ie you demonstrate little or no understanding of the key issues and risks, and do not reach reasonable conclusions as you have failed to apply the law to the facts.
* You do not refer to pertinent ethical issues and/or the SRA Principles and rules of professional conduct.

■ A STEPPED APPROACH TO CASE AND MATTER ANALYSIS

Case and matter analysis can be broken down into five basic steps:
1. Identify the problem and the client's goal.
2. Identify the legal issues.
3. Complete an assessment of facts, evidence and instructions.
4. Produce the relevant advice and options.
5. Assist with the decision-making process and the next steps.

We will now work through a sample question and break down the steps to complete a case and matter analysis. This stepped approach will assist you to meet the SRA's assessment criteria, which is crucial to success in the SRA SQE2 centralised assessment. Question 1 focuses on tort negligence and professional conduct.

■ QUESTION 1

Email to candidate

From: Partner
Sent: 15 March 202#
To: Candidate
Subject: Mrs Zoe Crawley

Yesterday I met a new client, Mrs Zoe Crawley, who was supported by her son, Jonah Crawley. ID has been obtained.

Zoe was quite upset when she visited and struggled to speak clearly. Her arm was in a cast, and she seemed to be in a lot of pain. She managed to explain that she needed some advice about bringing legal action against the person who caused her the injury.

Background information

Zoe is a retired nurse who is 52 years of age. She retired two years ago after she inherited a large sum of money from her father, Mr Robert Willerton. She is a widow, and her husband's name was Mr Samuel Crawley.

Zoe explained that retiring early has been the best thing that has ever happened to her. She has been able to pursue hobbies, which she never previously had time to do. She was keen to inform me that she particularly enjoys gardening and her new hobby, skiing! Jonah explained that Zoe has been skiing for the last year and she is very good at it.

The injury happened about a month ago when Zoe was on her way to the local gym. She was walking on a designated pedestrian pathway, adjacent to a public road. A speeding car veered off the road, mounted the curb and hit her.

An ambulance and the police were called (she does not know who made this call). Zoe is aware from the police that the driver, who she now knows is called Elliot James, was found to have been under the influence of alcohol, above the legal limit.

At the hospital it was confirmed that Zoe had a broken arm, two broken ribs and brain damage, namely dysarthria. Doctors at the hospital were surprised that Zoe had survived, and said that if she had been walking even slightly closer to the road, she would probably have died.

Zoe said that since the incident she has difficulty in speaking. This was very visible during the meeting. Her son explained that she has difficulty moving her mouth at times, her speech is significantly slower than it used to be and she slurs certain words. Zoe has speech and language therapy which she pays for privately. She is also paying for trauma therapy, because she keeps having nightmares about the incident.

Advice and analysis required

Zoe and Jonah would like advice about whether they can take legal action against Elliot James. They would prefer an option that causes the least amount of stress for Zoe.

I would like you to provide this analysis and advice for me to use as the basis of a letter to Zoe. When providing your advice, please remember that Zoe has no legal knowledge. She would like a brief explanation of the relevant law where appropriate, so please include this in your response.

Since the meeting, I have been informed by a colleague that Elliot James is one of the directors at James & Tuck Corporation. We successfully represented James & Tuck Corporation last year in respect of redundancies. I do not have the specific details because the file is password-protected by the employment law department. I am concerned that there may be a conflict of interest which prevents us from acting. I would like you to include this in your advice.

Please set out your advice and analysis on the following:

1. **Can Zoe pursue legal action against Elliot James? If so, what would you recommend is raised in a letter before action?**
2. **Can the firm continue to represent Zoe?**

Thanks
Partner

*   *   *

Let's address the first part of this question first: Can Zoe pursue legal action? What should be raised before action?

STEP 1   IDENTIFY THE PROBLEM AND THE CLIENT'S GOAL

In practice, case and matter analysis will often commence from a telephone call or meeting with a client. It can often be tempting to record all the information a client provides during an interview. However, whilst making a detailed attendance note may be helpful, it might not help you to assess the facts against the relevant legal framework.

It is crucial for a solicitor to pick out the key information so that they can give accurate advice and not be sidetracked by irrelevant facts.

HAVE A GO

Try to pick out the key facts from question 1.
1.   At this initial stage, focus on defining the problem and identifying Zoe's goal from her perspective.
2.   Remember that you should only select facts that are relevant and will assist you in providing advice.

Once you have completed this, see Table 1.3. It sets out which facts are relevant, and explains why those facts are important.

Table 1.3 Relevant facts in question 1

Relevant fact	Why is this relevant?
1. Zoe is retired.	You will not have to consider a loss of earnings when you consider what damages she may seek.
2. She was walking on a designated pedestrian pathway, adjacent to a public road.	Zoe was not walking in the middle of the road or acting recklessly.
3. A speeding car veered off the road, mounted the curb and hit her.	A standard is applied to the reasonably competent and experienced driver. If the driver was not adhering to the speed limit and was veering off the road, this could indicate reckless driving.
4. An ambulance and the police were called.	This could indicate that there are other witnesses. It would also be useful to find out from the client what action the police have taken, if any.
5. The driver was found to have been under the influence of alcohol, above the legal limit.	As with fact 3, a standard is applied to the reasonably competent and experienced driver. If there is evidence that the driver was under the influence of alcohol and above the legal limit, this can indicate a breach of that standard and therefore a breach of the duty of care a driver owes to other road users.
6. At the hospital it was confirmed that Zoe had a broken arm, two broken ribs and brain damage, namely dysarthria.	The hospital will have evidence of the injury the client has suffered because of the incident.
7. Effects on Zoe: • Since the incident she has difficulty in speaking … she has difficulty moving her mouth at times, her speech is significantly slower than it used to be and she slurs certain words. • Zoe has speech and language therapy which she pays for privately. • She is also paying for trauma therapy, because she keeps having nightmares about the incident.	This information will assist when quantifying quantum.

From these relevant facts, you should be able to identify the client's problem and their goal:
• Zoe has allegedly been injured due to Elliot James's reckless driving.
• Her goal is to obtain compensation for her injuries in the least stressful way.

Now that you have reviewed the relevant facts, look at this list of irrelevant facts from the question:
• Zoe enjoys gardening.
• She enjoys skiing.
• Zoe's husband has died.
• She inherited a large sum of money from her father.
• Zoe was on her way to the local gym.

These facts are not relevant to the legal issue and legislation. For example, Zoe enjoying gardening does not help you to establish whether or not she can take legal action against Elliot James. If you referred to all the facts in the email, or to irrelevant facts only, or if you did not refer to enough relevant facts, you would be deemed not competent by the SRA.

(You will note that there were a lot of irrelevant facts in this scenario. The number of irrelevant facts has been exaggerated for learning purposes, and it is unlikely the SQE2 assessment will contain so many.)

STEP 2 IDENTIFY THE LEGAL ISSUES

Once you have established the key facts, the problem and the client's goals, you should identify the legal issues and the relevant law, including a legal test if appropriate. This is where your FLK is crucial. The relevant law will not be given to you in the assessment, so it is important to keep your FLK up to date before the SQE2 centralised assessment.

Assessment technique

Start by determining whether the issue is contentious or non-contentious.

• Contentious matters involve a dispute. Disputes will often lead to litigation, which means you will need to analyse whether your client meets the relevant legal test to bring a case.
• Non-contentious approaches involve progressing matters without a dispute or litigation. You will need to analyse what the client must do in consideration of the law.

Do not assume that certain areas of law will always be contentious or non-contentious. Whilst property law, in particular conveyancing, is largely non-contentious, there will be occasions when the issue will be contentious, and the matter may progress to the Land Tribunal.

HAVE A GO

Read through question 1 and Table 1.3 again. Can you identify the legal issues and relevant legal elements?

Once you have done this, look at the list of key legal points below.

➥Key legal points: question 1

The relevant cause of action here is tort negligence, specifically a road traffic accident.

Tort negligence requires the following legal elements to be evidenced:
1.   duty
2.   breach of duty
3.   causation

4. remoteness
5. damages.

1. Duty

Remember from your FLK that all road users have a duty of care. Road users include drivers, cyclists, motorbike riders, passengers and pedestrians. Road users should avoid causing injury to others because of their actions or failure to act, where this can be reasonably anticipated. The standard of care in question 1 is that of a reasonably competent and experienced driver.

2. Breach of duty

Demonstrating a breach of duty depends very much on the facts. In practice, you would need to review the relevant legislation. For question 1, the facts indicate that the driver was (1) speeding/driving recklessly and (2) under the influence of alcohol. This would indicate a breach of duty. The driver might also have or face a criminal prosecution for this incident.

3. Causation

You should recall from your FLK that causation is based on the 'but for' test. We must ask, 'but for' the driver speeding/driving recklessly and being under the influence of alcohol, would he have hit Zoe with the car and caused her injuries?

4. Remoteness

We now need to consider the type of loss suffered and whether the consequences of the driver's actions were so far removed from the breach of duty as to have been unforeseeable by Zoe.

5. Damages

This is often referred to as quantifying the quantum. In other words, how much is the case worth in total, and is it worth pursuing? Remember that you have a duty to act in the client's best interests, and you should make your client aware if a case is not financially worthwhile to pursue. This is particularly relevant to the assessment criterion 'Apply the law comprehensively to the client's situation, identifying any ethical and professional conduct issues and exercising judgement to resolve them honestly and with integrity'. Damages for personal injury take the form of both general and special damages. Make sure you are clear on the difference between the two.

STEP 3 COMPLETE AN ASSESSMENT OF FACTS AND EVIDENCE

This is your opportunity to apply the facts to the law and analyse the strengths and weaknesses of your client's case. It might help you to identify 'good' facts which help your client's case, and 'bad' facts which might damage it.

Assessment technique

When you have established whether the matter is contentious or non-contentious, you will be able to focus your analysis.

- For contentious matters, you will be able to analyse which facts work in your favour for your legal argument and which are likely to weaken your case. This will enable you to assess the likelihood of success of an application to court, and form your advice.
- For non-contentious matters, you will be able to analyse the next steps or options, subject to the client meeting the legal test.

Once you have completed this, see the answer in Table 1.4.

Table 1.4 Assessment of facts in question 1

Legal element for the tort of negligence	Assessing the facts
1. Duty	**Good fact**: as a road user, Elliot James owes a duty of care to other road users. This means he owes a duty of care to Zoe, who was a pedestrian road user.
2. Breach of duty	**Good fact**: the police have confirmed to Zoe that Elliot James was under the influence of alcohol. This indicates a breach of duty. **Bad fact**: we do not know whether the police are intending to prosecute Elliot James for speeding or driving under the influence. If they do not intend to prosecute, this will weaken Zoe's case that there has been a breach of duty.
3. Causation	'But for' Elliot James speeding and being under the influence of alcohol, would he have hit Zoe with the car and caused her injuries? **Good fact**: we do not currently have any information that would suggest a break in the chain of causation.
4. Remoteness	As a result of the breach, Zoe has suffered a broken arm, two broken ribs and brain damage, namely dysarthria. She has difficulty moving her mouth at times, her speech is significantly slower than it used to be and she slurs certain words. **Good fact**: her son has confirmed the change since the incident and if required could provide a witness statement. Another good fact is that there will be clear evidence of the injury from hospital records/medical reports.
5. Damages	Zoe has speech and language therapy which she pays for privately. She is also paying for trauma therapy, because she keeps having nightmares about the incident. We will be claiming for both general and special damages. **Good fact**: Zoe should have invoices and other paperwork which can evidence the therapy expenses.

Let us now work through those facts and consider the possible evidence we can obtain to strengthen our case: see Table 1.5.

Table 1.5 Question 1: Evidence to obtain

Relevant facts	Evidence to obtain
Zoe was walking on a designated pedestrian pathway, adjacent to a public road. A speeding car veered off the road, mounted the curb and hit her.	- Photos of the location - Sketch plan of the location - CCTV footage - Photos of any damage to the car: this may be in a police accident report - Find out whether the driver had a dashcam which was taken by the police.
An ambulance and the police were called.	- Witness statements - Police accident report.
The driver was found to have been under the influence of alcohol, above the legal limit.	- Police accident report.
At hospital it was confirmed that Zoe had a broken arm, two broken ribs and brain damage, namely dysarthria.	- GP records/hospital records.
Since the incident Zoe has difficulty in speaking ... she has difficulty moving her mouth at times, her speech is significantly slower than it used to be and she slurs certain words. Zoe has speech and language therapy which she pays for privately. She is also paying for trauma therapy, because she keeps having nightmares about the incident.	- Medical report - Invoices for the speech and language therapy - Invoices for the trauma therapy.

STEP 4 PRODUCE THE RELEVANT ADVICE AND OPTIONS

We must now consider what options are available to the client. In the assessment, you will need to show that you can provide client-focused advice, which demonstrates an understanding of the problem from the client's perspective. You should consider the client's goals and then outline relevant options, including the advantages and disadvantages of those options.

Remember that your client might not meet the legal elements and therefore does not have a case to pursue. You will need to develop the valuable skill of considering alternative options which may achieve the client's objective without legal proceedings.

The three main options are:
- do nothing and walk away
- negotiation
- litigation.

However, further options/actions could also include:
- a letter of claim
- mediation
- Part 36 offer
- conciliation
- arbitration
- expert determination.

SQE 1 Functioning legal knowledge link

If you are unfamiliar with any of the terms in these lists, it is essential that you review your FLK from SQE1. You can revise your knowledge of these terms in *Revise SQE: Dispute Resolution*, *Revise SQE: Tort Law* and *Revise SQE: Contract Law*.

HAVE A GO

Now consider the lists of options in the context of question 1, and try to decide which are the most relevant to Zoe. Remember that you should evaluate the advantages and disadvantages of each option.
- Advantages are usually associated with saving time and costs.
- Disadvantages can include producing unenforceable agreements which are not binding.

Once you have prepared a list of relevant options and outlined the advantages and disadvantages, see Table 1.6.

Assessment technique

Start by thinking about what your client's underlying interest might be. Then compare that to the respondent's underlying interest.

Zoe has a variety of medical issues arising from the incident. She is currently undertaking therapy. She would like to receive damages. She would prefer an option that is going to cause her the least amount of stress. From the current information, and subject to obtaining the additional documents outlined in Table 1.5, she appears to have a strong case.

We do not know a lot about Elliot James, save that he is one of the directors at James & Tuck Corporation. Even though James & Tuck Corporation is not the defendant, it will be useful to complete a Companies House search against James & Tuck Corporation, to confirm that Elliot James is still a director and that the company is profitable: we need to consider whether Elliot James is worth suing. If he is still a director, there may be some ramifications to his reputation and that of the company if the public were aware that he drove under the influence of alcohol and hit Zoe with his car.

Table 1.6 Advantages and disadvantages of the three main options for the client in question 1

Option	Advantage	Disadvantage	Is this in Zoe's best interests?
Do nothing and walk away	- Zoe will be able to move on with her life.	- Zoe will not receive any damages.	Whilst this option would be the least stressful, Zoe is seeking damages. This option would not achieve her underlying interests.
Negotiation	- Less stressful than litigation. - Likely that Zoe will receive some damages. - This could be less time-consuming than court proceedings.	- This could be costly, depending on the duration of the negotiations. - This option depends on the co-operation of the defendant.	This option would be less stressful than litigation, and it is likely that Zoe will receive some damages. The damages might be less than what she would receive if she pursued litigation. However, the value may not be a problem for Zoe as she is already wealthy from her inheritance.
Litigation	- Zoe has a strong case. - No known time constraints.	- Costly. - Time-consuming. - Stressful. - Litigation risk.	This option will be stressful for Zoe. However, she does have a strong case and therefore litigation risk is low.

Code of Conduct for Solicitors, RELs and RFLs link

Full details of the SRA's Code of Conduct for Solicitors, RELs and RFLs are available on their website: www.sra.org.uk/solicitors/standards-regulations/code-conduct -solicitors/. This Code describes the standards of professionalism that are expected by the SRA (and the public) of solicitors who have been authorised by the SRA to provide legal services.

The Code applies to conduct and behaviour relating to legal practice. It creates a framework for ethical and competent practice, which will apply to your future career as a solicitor, regardless of your role or the environment/organisation in which you work.

A summary of the Code:

Code of Conduct for Solicitors, RELs and RFLs

1	Maintaining trust and acting fairly
2	Dispute resolution and proceedings before courts, tribunals and inquiries
3	Service and competence
4	Client money and assets

Business requirements

5.1–5.3	Referrals, introductions and separate businesses
5.4–5.6	Other business requirements

Conflict, confidentiality and disclosure

6.1–6.2	Conflict of interests
6.3–6.5	Confidentiality and disclosure
7	Cooperation and accountability

When you are providing services to the public or a section of the public

8.1	Client identification
8.2–8.5	Complaints handling
8.6–8.11	Client information and publicity

Rule 1.4 states that you must not mislead or attempt to mislead your clients, the court or others, either by your own actions or omissions, or being complicit in the acts or omissions of others (including your client). This is an important rule to bear in mind: it can often be difficult to tell clients that they have a weak case, but to mislead them into thinking they have a strong case may amount to a breach of this rule.

STEP 5 ASSIST WITH THE DECISION-MAKING PROCESS AND THE NEXT STEPS

Remember that your role is to advise, not to make the final decision. To advise Zoe, you need to ensure that your report to the partner includes an effective conclusion about her options and recommendations on how she should proceed, considering her best interests. As discussed above, the first option should be a letter of claim. See below for the correct protocol to follow.

Pre-Action Protocol for Personal Injury Claims

The Pre-Action Protocol for Personal Injury Claims recommends under paragraph 1.6 that before a letter of claim is sent, defendants should have three months to investigate and respond to a claim before proceedings are issued (although this is not always possible).

Per paragraph 3.1 the claimant or his legal representative may wish to notify a defendant and/or the insurer as soon as they know a claim is likely to be made, but before they are able to send a detailed letter of claim. The letter of notification should advise the defendant and/or the insurer of any relevant information that is available to assist with determining issues of liability/suitability of the claim for an interim payment and/or early rehabilitation under paragraph 3.2. Per paragraph 3.3 the letter of notification should be acknowledged within 14 days of receipt.

Per paragraph 5.2 the letter of claim should include the information described in the template at Annexe B1. The level of detail will need to be varied to suit the particular circumstances. In all cases, there should be sufficient information for the defendant to assess liability and to enable the defendant to estimate the likely size and heads of the claim without necessarily addressing the quantum in detail.

Per paragraph 5.3 the letter should contain a clear summary of the facts on which the claim is based together with an indication of the nature of any injuries suffered, and the way in which these impact on the claimant's day-to-day functioning and prognosis. Any financial loss incurred by the claimant should be outlined with an indication of the heads of damage to be claimed and the amount of that loss, unless this is impracticable.

Per paragraph 5.4 details of the claimant's National Insurance number and date of birth should be supplied to the defendant's insurer once the defendant has responded to the letter of claim and confirmed the identity of the insurer. This information should not be supplied in the letter of claim.

HAVE A GO

Try to compile a list of the next steps in relation to question 1.

It is important that your recommended next steps are relevant to Zoe's specific case. For example, recommending that details about funding are sent to the client is a very general suggestion, and unlikely to attract many marks if the question does not specifically ask you to deal with that.

Once you have done this, see our recommended next steps in the flow chart on page 17. On balance, it seems the best option for Zoe is to negotiate. This will be the least stressful option and it is also likely to result in her receiving some damages. Strategically it will be best to start by sending Elliot James a letter of claim and thereafter enter negotiations.

Assessment technique

Remember to distinguish what the client's next steps are and what the solicitor's next steps are. This will help to demonstrate your focus on the client and an understanding of the problem from their perspective: what you need to do to achieve the client's desired outcome, and not just from a legal perspective.

The firm might be unable to proceed until the client has provided certain information, such as photographic ID.

<table>
<tr><th style="text-align:center">Next steps for the firm</th><th style="text-align:center">Next steps for Zoe</th></tr>
<tr><td style="text-align:center">↓</td><td style="text-align:center">↓</td></tr>
<tr><td>Send a letter to Zoe within the next five working days. The letter should set out the advice contained in the report and highlight the options available to her.</td><td>Confirm how she would like to proceed following your recommendation to progress with negotiation, including whether she wishes to instruct the firm.</td></tr>
<tr><td style="text-align:center">↓</td><td style="text-align:center">↓</td></tr>
<tr><td>Upon confirmation of being instructed:</td><td>Inform her that if she wishes to instruct us, we will need her to provide:</td></tr>
<tr><td style="text-align:center">↓</td><td style="text-align:center">↓</td></tr>
<tr><td>

- Complete a Companies House search against James & Tuck Corporation.
- Prepare a letter of claim to send to the defendant, outlining the case and the intention to pursue legal action. Indicate a willingness to negotiate.

</td><td>

- Invoices for the speech and language therapy.
- Invoices for the trauma therapy.
- Medical records if she has them; if not, we can ask her to sign a form of authority so that the firm can obtain her medical records.
- Any documentation from the police, including an update on whether Elliot James has been criminally charged.

</td></tr>
</table>

Code of Conduct for Solicitors, RELs and RFLs link

Remember that as per the SRA's Code of Conduct rule 2.6, you must not waste the court's time. This includes progressing cases that do not have any legal merit. Without strong case and matter analysis skills, you may unintentionally breach the Code.

Now let us look at the second part of question 1: Can the firm continue to represent Zoe?

HAVE A GO

Now that we have gone through case and matter analysis for the first issue of question 1, apply the same five-step approach to the second part of the question, whether or not the firm can continue to represent Zoe.

To remind yourself of the details of the question, turn to page 7.

Once you have tried to complete this, compare your response with the notes below.

STEP 1 IDENTIFY THE PROBLEM AND THE CLIENT'S GOAL

The relevant facts are as follows:

Since the meeting, I have been informed by a colleague that Elliot James is one of the directors at James & Tuck Corporation. We successfully represented James & Tuck Corporation last year in respect of redundancies. I do not have the specific details because the file is password-protected by the employment law department.

STEP 2 IDENTIFY THE LEGAL ISSUES

Conflict of interest

The SRA's Principle 7 (act in the best interests of each client) is the principle most applicable in determining whether or not the firm can act for Zoe. There will be a conflict of interest if the firm's separate duties to act in the best interests of Zoe and James & Tuck Corporation do not coincide, and if this happens the firm will not be able to represent both clients. For there to be a conflict of interest, the firm must be currently acting, or intending to act, for Zoe *and* Elliot James.

Confidentiality

Section 6 of the Code for Solicitors (and the Code for Firms) sets out the rules regarding conflicts of interest and confidentiality. The firm has a duty to Zoe to disclose 'material information'. This must be information that is relevant to the specific retainer, and more than just passing interest. Material information would probably significantly impact the client's decision-making. If the information is not material information, the firm might be able to continue acting.

The question therefore becomes – is the James & Tuck Corporation employment case material information to Zoe's tort negligence claim?

STEP 3 COMPLETE AN ASSESSMENT OF FACTS, EVIDENCE AND INSTRUCTIONS

Table 1.7 assesses the facts of the legal issues in this part of question 1.

Table 1.7 Assessing the facts relating to the legal issue

Legal issue	Assessing the facts, evidence and instructions
Conflict of interest	**Good facts:** - The firm previously represented James & Tuck Corporation, not Elliot James as an individual. - The case seems to have concluded last year; James & Tuck Corporation does not appear to be a current client. However, this should be confirmed as a next step. - The firm represented James & Tuck Corporation last year in respect of redundancies. We know from question 1 that Zoe retired two years ago from her job as a nurse. It is unlikely that she was employed by the company.
Confidentiality	**Good facts:** - James & Tuck Corporation's employment case is unlikely to include material information to Zoe's tort negligence claim. - James & Tuck Corporation's employment case is password-protected, which will act as an information barrier to the person dealing with Zoe's case.

Additional information/evidence you might need to find out:
- Has the employment case concluded, or is there an ongoing appeal?
- Was Zoe party to the employment proceedings?
- Who at the firm instructed the employment law department?

STEP 4 PRODUCE THE RELEVANT ADVICE AND OPTIONS

It seems that the case concluded last year, and if so, James & Tuck Corporation will not be an existing client. In any event it is possible to distinguish Elliot James and James & Tuck Corporation.

It is unknown whether Elliot James or another director/member of staff instructed the firm on behalf of James & Tuck Corporation. It is also unknown what level of involvement Elliot James had in the employment law case.

The file is password-protected, which will act as an information barrier. The lack of access means that it is safe for the firm to represent Zoe.

There are only two options: either continue acting for Zoe or cease acting.

STEP 5 ASSIST WITH THE DECISION-MAKING PROCESS AND THE NEXT STEPS

The firm can continue acting for Zoe.

■ YOUR TURN

Now that we have worked through a stepped approach to case and matter analysis, try to complete a report to a supervisor based on question 1.
- Refer to the SRA's assessment criteria for case and matter analysis (pages 3–4) while you compile your report.
- Use the five steps on pages 8–15 as a structure for your report.
- Do not forget to time yourself. Timings are important: you will need to prepare and write your answer in 60 minutes.

EVALUATING YOUR ANSWER

Once you have attempted completing the report, mark it yourself against the SQE2 case and matter analysis criteria. Do you think your attempt met the threshold?

Now compare your attempt with the two sample answers below. A circled number indicates that commentary is provided for this part of the answer. The commentary will explain whether or not the sample answer is likely to meet the SQE2 standard threshold.

■ SAMPLE ANSWER 1 TO QUESTION 1

Zoe was injured a month ago: a speeding car veered off the road, mounted the pavement and hit her, while she was walking on a designated pedestrian pathway next to a public road. She was taken to hospital where it was confirmed that she had suffered a broken arm, two broken ribs and brain damage (dysarthria). The incident has significantly affected Zoe's speech. She is paying for speech and language therapy, as well as trauma therapy for nightmares she has about the incident.

The police attended the incident and have subsequently confirmed that the driver, Elliot James, was driving the vehicle under the influence of alcohol (above the legal limit).

Zoe retired two years ago, having inherited a large sum of money from her father, and is seeking a legal remedy which causes her the least amount of stress.

Elliot James is a director at James & Tuck Corporation. The firm represented James & Tuck Corporation last year in respect of redundancies. The file is password-protected by the employment law department and details of that matter are unknown. ❶

1. **Can Zoe pursue legal action against Elliot James? If so, what would you recommend is raised in a letter before action?**

Zoe can pursue legal action against Elliot James. ❷
- The incident occurred a month ago, which means that any claim will be within the limitation period.
- As a **road user**, Elliot James owed a **duty of care** to Zoe, a pedestrian road user. It would appear Elliot James has **breached** that duty of care by driving under the influence of alcohol above the legal limit.
- There does not appear to be any breach in the chain of **causation**. It is likely that Elliot James would *not* have hit Zoe with his car, had he not been speeding and under the influence of alcohol.
- Zoe's son has confirmed that the injuries described above were caused by the incident, thus the loss suffered and consequences of the driver's actions were so far **removed** from the breach of duty as to have been unforeseeable by Zoe. Evidence of the injuries she has suffered should be obtained from the hospital and her therapists. ❸ Zoe should claim for both general and special **damages**. ❹

On the current information, Zoe's case is strong. She could commence court proceedings against Elliot James. However, considering that she is seeking the least stressful option, it would be preferable to negotiate a settlement outside court. ❺

To initiate negotiations, we should send a letter before action. The Pre-Action Protocol for Personal Injury Claims sets out best practice for the contents of a letter of claim (also known as a letter before action). ❻ For this case, the letter of claim should include:
a. A clear summary of the facts on which the claim is based (which is set out above), and a summary of the reasons Zoe is alleging fault (which will be based upon the information the police have given her).
b. A description of the injuries that Zoe has suffered because of the incident and the impact of the injuries on her day-to-day life. We may need to take further instructions on this, as we are currently only aware of the impact on her speech and the nightmares she is suffering.
c. The financial loss Zoe has suffered, including the types of damage available to her and monetary value of damages claimed where possible, which will include the cost of therapy.
d. Details such as the hospital name, address and reference number. We will need to confirm whether we have or are trying to obtain the police report. We should request the identity of Elliot James's car insurer and provide a list of documents (for example, evidence from the hospital) which we believe are relevant to Elliot James and/or his legal representation. ❼

However, before sending a letter before action, it would be advisable to do the following:
- Confirm whether the police intend to prosecute Elliot James for speeding or driving under the influence. If they do not, this could weaken Zoe's case. If they do, we should obtain evidence of that intention to prosecute.
- Obtain evidence from the hospital and therapists. We will need to obtain further instructions from Zoe about which hospital and therapists she attended/attends. We will also need the therapists' invoices to assist with calculating damages.
- Obtain further instructions from Zoe about the impact of her injuries on her day-to-day life. It will also be useful to obtain a witness statement from her son regarding the impact of the injuries since the incident. ❽

Once we have all of the above information, we should complete a further case and matter analysis to advise Zoe on the strength of her case.

2. Can the firm continue to represent Zoe?

The firm would be unable to represent Zoe if our duty to act in the best interests of Zoe (SRA Principle 7) conflicted with our duty to act in the best interests of the James & Tuck Corporation conflict. For there to be a conflict of interest we must be currently acting, or intending to act, for both Zoe and Elliot James as individuals. However, the firm represented James & Tuck Corporation, not Elliot James; also, James & Tuck Corporation's case concluded last year and the company might not be a current client. As such it is unlikely that there will be a conflict with our duty to act in Zoe's best interests. **⑨**

The firm would also be unable to represent Zoe if there was a risk that we would breach our duty of confidentiality per section 6 of the Code for Solicitors (and the Code for Firms). We have a duty to Zoe to disclose material information that is relevant to the specific retainer and more than just passing interest. Information is material where it significantly impacts the client's decision-making. If the information we have is not material, we may represent Zoe. It seems unlikely that the James & Tuck Corporation employment case last year will include material information to Zoe's tort negligence claim. There is also a password protecting the files, which maintains James & Tuck Corporation's confidentiality at the firm. Therefore, it is unlikely that the firm will breach any confidentiality rules, and can continue to represent Zoe. **⑩**

We may wish to confirm with our employment law department that the case is concluded and there is no ongoing appeal. **⑪**

COMMENTARY

① The first four paragraphs provide an accurate summary of the most relevant background information. The summary includes information relevant to establishing whether there was a duty of care owed – Zoe was a pedestrian so is deemed as a road user. The information further confirms that the duty Elliot James owed to other road users was breached due to being intoxicated and speeding. The candidate describes Zoe's injuries and summarises her financial position and overall goal. It is important to set out these facts at the onset, as they form the basis and structure of the advice provided below.

② The initial sentence effectively concludes the client's position. The partner reviewing the case and matter analysis report will need a clear, concise indication of whether the client has a worthwhile case right from the outset.

③ The points in this list correctly identify that Zoe can pursue legal action against Elliot James based on his breach of the duty of care he, as a road user, owed her, a pedestrian, and by driving under the influence of alcohol. This establishes the foundational elements of negligence: duty, breach, causation and damage. The answer effectively addresses the chain of causation, indicating no breach in the chain and linking Elliot James's actions directly to Zoe's injuries. However, it could be strengthened by discussing the 'but for' test to provide a more comprehensive analysis of causation. It is also noted that evidence from the hospital and therapists will be crucial in substantiating Zoe's injuries, which is appropriate. The recommendation to gather further evidence from Zoe and her therapists demonstrates thoroughness.

④ The candidate rightly suggests that Zoe should claim both general and special damages. However, this answer could be enhanced by providing examples of general damages (ie as compensation for pain and suffering) and special damages (ie to cover medical expenses and therapy costs).

5 The candidate correctly advises that, given Zoe's desire to avoid stress, negotiation and settlement are preferable to litigation. This aligns with the client's interests and demonstrates an appreciation of the practicalities of legal proceedings.

6 The suggestion to send a letter before action, in accordance with the Pre-Action Protocol for Personal Injury Claims, is appropriate and a procedural requirement. This demonstrates an understanding of legal protocol.

7 The proposed content of the letter before action is comprehensive and covers the necessary elements, such as the facts, allegations of fault, injuries, financial loss and relevant documents. This demonstrates a thorough understanding of pre-action procedures.

8 The advice to check whether the police intend to prosecute Elliot James and to obtain relevant evidence before proceeding is practical. This shows a strategic approach to strengthening Zoe's case.

9 The candidate correctly references the SRA Principle 7 to act in the best interests of the client, demonstrating a sound understanding of professional conduct rules. The analysis of conflict of interest correctly distinguishes between representing Zoe and representing James & Tuck Corporation, noting that since the corporation is no longer a current client, there is unlikely to be a conflict.

10 The candidate appropriately addresses the duty of confidentiality, referring to the Code for Solicitors. There is a correct assessment of the risk of breaching confidentiality, and a conclusion that this is unlikely, given the password protection and the nature of the previous case.

11 This is a prudent suggestion. It demonstrates an ability to exercise judgement to resolve matters with honesty and integrity, part of the SQE2 assessment criteria for case and matter analysis.

Does this answer meet the threshold?

This answer is likely to meet the SRA's threshold criteria. The candidate clearly identifies the relevant facts and the advice is client-focused, demonstrating an understanding that Zoe's goal is to achieve a positive outcome in the least stressful way. The language is appropriate for the reader, a partner at the firm, who will be familiar with legal terminology, such as 'material information'.

The law has been correctly applied to the client's situation. Ethical and professional conduct issues have been considered, and attempts have been made to resolve them honestly and with integrity by seeking further information as a next step.

The answer provides a solid foundation for Zoe's legal options and the firm's ability to represent her, demonstrating a good understanding of negligence and professional conduct rules.

Whilst we would state that this answer meets the threshold, it could be improved by elaborating on questions that should be put to Zoe when obtaining further instructions. The candidate could also go into further detail in discussing the different types of damages in personal injury claims, such as general and special damages. These additional aspects would make the answer more comprehensive and informative.

Now let's consider the second sample answer to question 1.

■ SAMPLE ANSWER 2 TO QUESTION 1

Zoe got hurt a while back when she got hit by a fast car that drove off the road and hit her on the path. ❶

She went to the hospital and had some broken ribs and brain damage called dysarthria. Zoe has trouble talking, sometimes can't move her mouth right, and speaks really slow and slurs her words. She is paying out of pocket for speech therapy and trauma therapy because she has bad dreams about what happened. ❷

The police came to the scene and later said the driver, James Elliot, was drunk. Zoe is retired because she got a lot of money from her dad and wants to take legal action with the least stress. Elliot James is a big shot at James & Tuck Corporation. Last year, the firm worked with the company on lay-offs, but the details are locked and no one knows what's in them. ❸

1.   Can Zoe sue Elliot James? What should be in the letter before action?

Yes, Zoe can sue Elliot James. He should have been careful as a driver but wasn't because he was drunk. There's no reason to think anything else caused the accident; he hit her because he was drunk and driving too fast. ❹

Zoe's son said she got those injuries from the accident. We can get proof from the hospital and her therapists. Zoe should ask for damages for her pain and therapy costs. Since she wants less stress, it's better to settle out of court. ❺

To start, we send a letter before action, using the Pre-Action Protocol for Personal Injury Claims. The letter needs to include the facts, why Zoe thinks Elliot is at fault (based on what the police said), her injuries and their effects on her life, and her therapy costs. Include hospital details, check if we have or need the police report, ask for Elliot's car insurer, and list relevant documents. ❻

Before sending the letter, check if the police charge Elliot for drunk driving or speeding. If not, it makes Zoe's case weaker. If they will, get the police report. Also, get evidence from hospital and therapists, and more details from Zoe about injuries and therapy invoices. A statement from her son about her condition since the would also help. Once we have this info, we can see how strong Zoe's case is. ❼

2.   Can the firm still represent Zoe?

The firm can't represent Zoe if there's a conflict of interest with Elliot James. Since Elliot James isn't a client anymore, there's probably no conflict.

We have to tell Zoe any 'material information' that affects her decisions. If the info from last year's layoffs is material, we can represent Zoe. The case files are password-protected, so James & Tuck's info stays confidential. So, it's unlikely we'll break confidentiality rules, and we can keep representing Zoe. ❽

COMMENTARY

❶ This initial sentence is not sufficiently specific and is poorly written. The location is also not correct. The candidate must specifically state where Zoe was when she was hit by the car, as it affects whether or not she was acting as a road user at the time of the incident, and therefore the duty of care owed to her. It is also not clear when the incident occurred, which is relevant when establishing whether a claim would be within the limitation period.

2 This is not professionally phrased and is missing key information such as the injury to her arm. It also does not clearly establish that these injuries have occurred as a result of the incident.

3 This paragraph is also poorly phrased. Elliot James is incorrectly named James Elliot in the first sentence. There is not enough information about the police. The language is not appropriate in a written report to a partner, such as stating that the client 'got a lot of money from her dad', describing Elliot James as a big shot and using the term 'lay-offs' instead of redundancies. Additionally, the last sentence is incorrect because the employment law department in the firm *does* know what is in the James & Tuck Corporation case file.

4 This paragraph is alluding to the legal test which needs to be satisfied, but it lacks important legal terminology and discussion of all elements of the legal test. There is no clear mention of the duty Elliot James owes as a reasonable driver. The paragraph is also quite repetitive in nature, twice mentioning that Elliot was drunk.

5 This paragraph gives insufficient information about the type of damages that the firm should be seeking to claim. Moreover, stating that it would be better to settle out of court does not help the reader to know whether Zoe has a strong case, or the process of settling out of court. It would be better to specify that this can be accomplished by initiating negotiations through sending a letter before action.

6 It is positive that the Pre-Action Protocol has been referenced. However, the elements that need to be included in the letter are not sufficiently detailed. When mentioning why Zoe thinks Elliot James is at fault, the candidate should refer to the duty owed by Elliot, and how he has breached such duty. What is meant by hospital details is also unclear.

7 Some of the sentences in this paragraph appear to have words missing, which impacts its readability. It also talks about getting evidence such as the police report, but it is not clear who should be getting these things. Is this something the firm will want Zoe to obtain, or something the firm will request on her behalf? This is an example of where the sentences have been made too concise, so that it is not clear who is doing what as a next step.

8 The paragraphs contain incorrect information on whether the firm can continue to represent Zoe if it has material information from the previous case. It has been incorrectly recorded that Elliot James was the firm's client, when in fact it was the company James & Tuck Corporation who was the client. The language in the paragraph is not appropriately formal. An example is where information is shortened to 'info'. In the final paragraph, the candidate has accurately recorded that the file is password-protected and reached the correct legal advice, but their explanation could have been clearer and more formal. Remember that this is a note for the partner, and should contain appropriate legal language.

Does this answer meet the threshold?

This answer identifies some relevant facts, although it omits some information which significantly impacts the case. For example, exclusion of the arm injury will affect the damages sum being claimed. Some facts have also been recorded incorrectly, which impacts the accuracy of the advice.

The answer does provide some client-focused advice which demonstrates an understanding of the problem from the client's perspective, such as recognising that it will be less stressful for Zoe for the case to be settled outside court. However, the way that the report is written is not consistently concise or clear, and uses unacceptable language in places.

The candidate refers to the correct law but at a basic level, and key elements of the legal test have been excluded. On balance, this answer is unlikely to meet the SQE2 assessment criteria threshold.

The SRA can assess any of the areas on the SQE2 specification. Below is another example of how a different part of the specification – business organisations, rules and procedures – could arise in the context of SQE2 case and matter analysis.

■ QUESTION 2

Email to candidate

From: Partner
Sent: 1 April 202#
To: Candidate
Subject: Hasan Wallick

Background information

Two weeks ago, I spoke to a new client called Hasan Wallick. He was away on business and only available for a telephone appointment.

Mr Wallick advised me that he sought to buy shares in a company called Mersser LTD. He was intending to buy the shares from an existing shareholder called Jennifer. He did not remember her surname.

Mr Wallick explained that four years ago he paid his nephew's university fees. His nephew is now working full-time and has started to pay him back. Rather than paying Mr Wallick directly, his nephew will make the payment on account to the firm for the shares. I explained that we would not need funds on account until closer to the purchase, but Mr Wallick insisted that it would be easier for everyone if the firm keeps the money on account until the shares have been purchased.

Mr Wallick has since provided me with his ID over email and I have been able to confirm his identity.

I provided Mr Wallick with the firm's payment details and we received a payment from his nephew two days after the telephone call.

Last week I received a telephone call from Mr Wallick, who advised that as Jennifer was asking for more money, he has decided to back out of the deal. Mr Wallick asked that I return the money to him, which I did via BACS.

I have now received an email from the firm's money laundering reporting officer. He is concerned that I might have committed a criminal offence.

Advice and analysis required

I would like you to review the file and complete a case and matter analysis on whether legal action can be brought against me.

Please set out your advice and analysis on the following issues:

1   **Can legal action be brought against me under the Proceeds of Crime Act 2002?**
2   **If so, what are the ramifications?**

Thanks

Partner

* * *

■ YOUR TURN

Have a go at answering question 2: try to complete a report for the supervisor.
- Remember to refer to the SRA's assessment criteria on pages 3–4.
- Structure your report using the five steps outlined on pages 8–15.
- Timings are important: you will need to prepare and write your report in 60 minutes.

SQE 1 Functioning legal knowledge link

For further discussion of money laundering red flags, search the Law Society website at www.lawsociety.org.uk. If you need to review your knowledge of this area, see **Revise SQE: Business Law and Practice**.

EVALUATING YOUR ANSWER

When you have attempted the question, mark it yourself against the SQE2 case and matter analysis criteria. Do you think your attempt met the threshold standard?

Now compare your attempt with the following key legal points and two sample answers to question 2. A circled number indicates that commentary is provided for this part of the answer. The commentary will explain whether or not the sample is likely to meet the standard SQE2 threshold.

➡️Key legal points: question 2

The legal focus of this question is money laundering offences, which are set out in the Proceeds of Crime Act 2002.

To commit a **direct offence**, the solicitor must have had knowledge or suspicion of money laundering.

The Proceeds of Crime Act 2002 states that the following actions are direct offences:
- Section 327: to conceal, disguise, convert or transfer the proceeds of crime, or to remove the proceeds of crime from the jurisdiction of England and Wales.
- Section 328: to enter, or become concerned in an arrangement, in which the person knows or suspects the retention, use or control of the proceeds of crime.
- Section 329: to acquire, use or possess the proceeds of crime.

To commit an **indirect offence**, the solicitor would be taking steps to move money/property, or enable an individual to cover their tracks which may prejudice an investigation.

The following actions are indirect offences under the Proceeds of Crime Act 2002:
- Sections 330–2: to fail to report a suspected offence.
- Sections 333A–D: to tip off the client about suspicions of money laundering, and this prejudices any investigation.

■ SAMPLE ANSWER 1 TO QUESTION 2

Two weeks ago, you had a telephone appointment with a new client, Mr Wallick, who expressed an intention to purchase shares from an existing shareholder, Jennifer, whose surname he could not recall. Mr Wallick arranged for his nephew to directly transfer the funds to our firm to facilitate the share purchase. Despite your explanation that the funds would not be needed immediately, Mr Wallick insisted on payment being made straight away and we received payment from his nephew two days after the call. Subsequently, Mr Wallick decided to withdraw from the purchase and requested the return of his funds, which you facilitated via BACS. You have now been contacted by the firm's money laundering reporting officer (MLRO), who is concerned that you may have committed a criminal offence. ❶

1.   Can legal action be brought against you under the Proceeds of Crime Act 2002?

Legal action could potentially be brought against you under the Proceeds of Crime Act 2002 for committing an indirect offence. ❷

The Proceeds of Crime Act 2002 requires legal professionals to conduct proper due diligence and report suspicious activities. Offences can be committed either directly or indirectly.

Direct money laundering offences under Proceeds of Crime Act 2002 include:
- Section 327: Concealing, disguising, converting, transferring, or removing criminal property.
- Section 328: Entering into or becoming concerned in an arrangement which one knows, or suspects facilitates the acquisition, retention, use, or control of criminal property by or on behalf of another person.
- Section 329: Acquiring, using, or having possession of criminal property.

For a direct money laundering offence under the Proceeds of Crime Act 2002 to be established, you must have had knowledge or been suspicious that the funds were the proceeds of crime. ❸

Based on the information provided, there is no indication that you had knowledge or suspicion that the funds were derived from criminal activity. You did verify Mr Wallick's identity. ❹

However, there were some warning signs which should have been considered:
a.   Mr Wallick's instructions were vague at times. The lack of full identification details for the seller (Jennifer) should have warranted additional verification steps to ensure validity.
b.   The funds were provided from Mr Wallick's nephew, a third party, which is unusual and required closer scrutiny.
c.   Although you advised Mr Wallick that funds were not required immediately, he insisted on transferring the money, which is atypical and should have prompted further investigation.
d.   The sudden breakdown of the purchase and the return of funds directly to the client rather than the nephew should have been more closely questioned. ❺

You will have committed an indirect money laundering offence under the Proceeds of Crime Act 2002 if you prevent that individual from taking action to move money/property, or take other steps which either cover their tracks or may prejudice an investigation. This does not seem to have occurred thus far. ❻

You will also have committed an indirect money laundering offence if you do not disclose to the appropriate authorities that you know or suspect, or have reasonable grounds to know or suspect, that Mr Wallick is engaged in money laundering. You should immediately, with the assistance of the MLRO, send a Serious Activity Report to the National Crime Agency about the suspected money laundering. Only if you make this disclosure will you have a defence to the offence. Immediate corrective actions and full cooperation with the MLRO and regulatory bodies are essential to mitigate potential legal and professional repercussions. **❼**

2. If so, what are the ramifications?

If you fail either to report the suspicious activity or to conduct appropriate due diligence, you could face criminal liability including imprisonment, a fine or both.

It is likely that you will also face professional consequences. A breach of anti-money laundering regulations can lead to disciplinary actions from the Solicitors Regulation Authority. This could result in a fine, suspension or even being struck off the roll of solicitors.

Finally, being implicated in a money laundering investigation can severely damage your professional reputation, potentially resulting in loss of clients and business opportunities. **❽**

COMMENTARY

❶ The answer effectively identifies and highlights the relevant facts of the case that raise potential legal and compliance issues under the Proceeds of Crime Act 2002, including:
- the initial conversation and intention to buy shares
- the involvement of Mr Wallick's nephew in the payment process
- the unusual insistence on transferring funds immediately
- the withdrawal from the deal and request for return of funds
- the communication from the firm's Money Laundering Reporting Officer (MLRO).

❷ This initial sentence effectively states the partner's position. The partner reviewing the case and matter analysis report will need a clear, concise indication of the position right from the outset.

❸ This paragraph correctly outlines the possible direct legal offences which could have been committed. It also discusses the required knowledge which the partner should have had for the offence to have been committed as defined by s 340(3) of the Proceeds of Crime Act 2002.

❹ This paragraph correctly applies the law to the facts and concludes that the partner is not likely to have committed a direct offence.

❺ This list highlights the red flags that should have been picked up by the solicitor. The points are laid out in a logical fashion, and the candidate demonstrates a thorough analysis of the events.

❻ This paragraph appropriately explains the legal test for an indirect offence to have been committed. The candidate correctly applies the test to the current scenario and concludes from the evidence that no such offence has been committed.

❼ The answer provides comprehensive advice that acknowledges the client's concerns and outlines the legal implications. It also provides the next steps to be undertaken.

❽ This section comprehensively covers the legal aspects, including potential breaches of the Proceeds of Crimes Act 2002, criminal liability, professional consequences and reputational damage. It also addresses the need for proper due diligence and reporting suspicious activities, highlighting ethical and professional conduct issues.

Does this answer meet the threshold?

The answer is well structured, making it easy to follow and understand. The language is clear, precise and appropriate, relevant facts are effectively identified and highlighted, and the advice is client-focused. The legal application is accurate and comprehensive. Ethical and professional conduct issues are addressed, with practical recommendations.

The answer is likely to meet the SQE2 assessment criteria, although it could be improved in some areas. For example:
- There could be more explicit emphasis on the partner's goals and perspective to enhance the client-focused advice.
- Specific examples of enhanced due diligence practices could be included, which would strengthen the practical aspect of the recommendations.
- There could be discussion of mitigating factors, to offer a more nuanced view on the likely criminal implications.

On balance, this answer is likely to meet the SQE2 criteria threshold.

Now let's consider the second sample answer to question 2.

■ SAMPLE ANSWER 2 TO QUESTION 2

Two weeks ago, you spoke to a new client, Hasan Wallick, via telephone as he was away on business. Mr Wallick intended to buy shares in a company from an existing shareholder named Jennifer. **❶**

Mr Wallick provided his ID via email, which you did not verify further as you trusted him. Two days after the call, we received the payment from his nephew. Last week, Mr Wallick contacted us to confirm that he decided to back out of the deal because Jennifer was asking for more money. Mr Wallick requested the return of the funds, which you did via BACS without any further checks. Later, you received an email from the firm's money laundering reporting officer (MLRO), who expressed concerns that you might have committed a criminal offence. **❷**

Under the Proceeds of Crime Act 2002, money laundering involves hiding or transferring illegal funds. The payment received from Mr Wallick's nephew seemed legitimate, so I don't believe there was any wrongdoing. **❸**

If the money was illegal, simply placing it in the firm's account and then returning it shouldn't be an issue. Possessing the funds temporarily doesn't seem like a problem unless the money is obviously criminal property. **❹**

In my opinion, there is no need to investigate the source of the funds since they came from a family member repaying a debt. If the funds were criminal, the worst that could happen would be a minor fine. The MLRO's concerns are probably unfounded, and there is no need to report anything to the National Crime Agency. The firm's reputation and compliance training are not affected by this incident, and there is no need to change our procedures. The matter should be closed without any further action. **❺**

COMMENTARY

① The answer fails to correctly identify and focus on relevant facts. For example, it does not clearly address the significance of the funds being paid by the nephew, nor does it recognise the importance of verifying the source of the funds.

② Whilst the language is clear, this paragraph lacks the necessary precision and depth. It fails to accurately explain the legal concepts and implications, and it includes assumptions without proper legal backing, so that it is misleading. The paragraph also contains inaccurate information. For example, the partner did not state that no further checks were completed on the ID, or that they trusted the client.

③ There is a significant lack of legal analysis which impacts the validity of the case and matter analysis. The candidate is not actually answering the questions posed by the partner. In contrast to sample answer 1, this answer does not include headings, and it lacks a clear structure to address the two parts of the question.

④ The paragraph contains significant legal errors. It dismisses the need for verifying the source of funds, and incorrectly assumes that placing and returning potentially illegal funds is not a problem. This demonstrates a failure to apply the Proceeds of Crime Act 2002 correctly.

⑤ The paragraph is not sufficiently detailed and overlooks key legal and ethical issues. It fails to consider the importance of anti-money laundering regulations and the ethical duty to report suspicious transactions. The conclusion that the matter should be closed without further action is incorrect and shows poor judgement.

Does this answer meet the threshold?

The candidate demonstrates several areas of incompetence, including failure to identify relevant facts, provide client-focused advice, use precise language or apply the law correctly and comprehensively.

Sample answer 2 does not address the potential red flags that might arise from the source and nature of these funds. It also incorrectly suggests that no further action is necessary and does not consider the client's need for protection against possible legal repercussions. If anything, the advice is putting the partner in a precarious position which might have serious consequences for their career.

The answer does not consider the importance of compliance with anti-money laundering regulations from the client's perspective, and it lacks the necessary depth and accuracy for the SQE2 assessment. The incorrect legal analysis combined with a lack of consideration for ethical obligations indicate a lack of professional competency and judgement. This answer is unlikely to meet the SQE2 assessment criteria threshold.

■ KEY POINT CHECKLIST

This chapter has covered the following key knowledge points:
* The SQE2 assessment criteria for case and matter analysis, and applying it in the context of professional conduct issues regarding conflicts of interest and money laundering.
* A stepped approach and suggested structure for approaching an SQE2 case and matter analysis question.
* Sample answers that show what is either likely or unlikely to meet the Day One Solicitor competency.

■ SUMMARY AND REFLECTION

The key to success in the SQE2 case and matter analysis assessment lies in effectively applying legal principles to the facts of a case, and critically evaluating the facts and evidence to assess risk. It is essential that you are able to identify which facts are crucial and recognise any gaps in the information provided.

To excel in this assessment, you need to do the following:
- **Apply legal tests**: demonstrate a thorough understanding of the relevant legal tests and apply them accurately to the facts provided.
- **Evaluate facts and evidence**: assess the significance of each fact and piece of evidence, determining their impact on the legal outcome.
- **Identify missing information**: recognise any information gaps that could affect your analysis, and understand the implications of these gaps.
- **Assess risk**: evaluate the potential risks involved in the case and advise accordingly, considering both legal and practical perspectives.
- **Think critically**: use critical thinking skills to analyse complex scenarios and provide clear, reasoned advice.

Before proceeding to the next chapter, take some time to reflect on your current level of competence in these areas. Consider what aspects you may need to improve and whether you feel completely confident in your case and matter analysis skills. Identifying your strengths and areas for development will help focus your efforts and enhance your performance in the SQE2 assessment.

2

Legal research

■ INTRODUCTION TO LEGAL RESEARCH

This chapter deals with the written skill of legal research. Whilst you might have some experience completing legal research in practice or during undergraduate study, this does not mean that you know how to meet the criteria set by the SRA. It is crucial to focus your revision on what the SRA's expectations are of a Day One Solicitor and how you will be examined in the SQE2 assessment.

This chapter explains what legal research is and why it is an important legal skill for a solicitor. It then explores how legal research is assessed under SQE2. You might notice that this skill is examined differently from how you might complete an everyday research exercise in practice. It is also different from the legal research assessment in the Legal Practice Course, where the focus was the journey to find the answer.

Next, the chapter will consider the criteria against which you will be assessed in the legal research SQE2 assessment. This will be followed by a detailed commentary of that assessment criteria. The chapter then demonstrates a stepped approach to legal research in the context of wills and intestacy, probate administration and practice (question 1). We have provided two sample answers for you to scrutinise.

Thereafter, you will have the opportunity to practise your own legal research skills in question 2, which is in the context of business practice, and produce a response. There are two sample answers that you can consider and use to reflect on your own answer.

WHAT IS LEGAL RESEARCH, AND WHY IS IT AN IMPORTANT SKILL FOR A SOLICITOR?

Legal research is a fundamental skill for solicitors. The law is continuously evolving, and you need to make sure that your knowledge is up to date so that you can give your client accurate legal advice.

You cannot always trust an online search engine to provide the correct legal information. You need to be able to use the right resources – **primary** and **secondary** sources (see Table 2.1) – to find the correct information.

If you are unable to navigate resources with confidence and accuracy, this may cost you time and your reputation. It is therefore important to master this skill as early as possible in your legal career for long-term benefits.

Table 2.1 Defining primary and secondary sources

What is a primary source?	What is a secondary source?
A primary source is the law. Primary sources include: • legislation • procedure rules • case law. Primary sources are often more difficult to understand due to the difficult legal language used. However, you must refer to them and use them, because they are the authority on what the law states.	A secondary source is an analysis of the law (the primary sources) which has been completed by someone else. It usually includes detailed explanations of the law. Examples of secondary sources: • *Halsbury's Laws of England* – a legal encyclopaedia which includes useful footnotes referencing the relevant legislation or case law. • Practitioner and academic textbooks – these will include legal explanations. • Journal articles – they usually include a commentary on the law.

HOW IS LEGAL RESEARCH ASSESSED IN SQE2?

For the legal research assessment, you will complete a 60-minute computer-based assessment. The SQE2 written centralised assessments take place over three half-days. You will be assessed on your legal research skills on each day:
• Day one – in the context of dispute resolution or criminal litigation.
• Day two – in the context of property practice or wills and intestacy, probate administration and practice.
• Day three – in the context of business organisations, rules and procedures.

You will be given an email from a partner that will include the factual background and problem you need to solve. As a competent Day One Solicitor, you will be required to investigate the situation and produce a written research note to a partner setting out the advice that they should provide to the client.

You will not have access to online resources, such as Lexis+, Westlaw or Practical Law, during the assessment. Instead, you will be given a mixture of primary and secondary sources that you need to analyse to find the answer to the problem posed. You should be strategic with your time because not every source will be relevant to the client's problem. You are being tested on your ability to identify which sources *are* relevant.

Your research note should also include the legal reasoning for your advice and which sources you relied upon to give that advice. As the focus of the research note is to provide advice to the client's problem and the legal reasoning behind this advice, you do not need to produce a legal research trail.

The subject matter of the legal research will be within the broad heading of the practice area in which the assessment is set (such as property practice or dispute resolution), which means it may be outside the scope of the SQE2 FLK. This will put your legal research skills to the test.

To pass the SQE2 assessment, you must demonstrate that you can meet the SRA's standard of competency of a Day One Solicitor. To remind yourself of the criteria, see Table 1.2 on page 3. You need to have sufficient knowledge to be competent to practise. The Day One Solicitor realistically will not know everything, which is why legal research is such a fundamental skill: it is expected that after a client interview has been held, a competent solicitor will be able to look up detail they did not know and report back to the client.

For the SQE2 assessment, you are not expected to know or address detail that a Day One Solicitor would have to look up, unless you have been provided with that detail as part of the assessment materials. Legal materials will only be provided where it is considered that a Day One Solicitor would need to refer to those materials.

■ ASSESSMENT CRITERIA AND COMMENTARY

As you prepare your answer in the SQE2 assessment for legal research, remember that it will be judged against the following criteria:

SQE2 legal research assessment criteria

Skills assessment criteria

1. Identify and use relevant sources and information.
2. Provide client-focused advice that addresses the client's problem.
3. Use clear, precise, concise and acceptable language.

Application of law assessment criteria

4. Apply the law correctly to the client's situation.
5. Apply the law comprehensively to the client's situation, identifying any ethical and professional conduct issues and exercising judgement to resolve them honestly and with integrity.

Let's look more closely at each point in these criteria, and explore the SRA's standard of competency as detailed in their performance indicators for SQE2 legal research.

SKILLS ASSESSMENT CRITERIA

1. Identify and use relevant sources and information

It may seem obvious that to complete legal research, you need to use sources relevant to the question. However, when you are not very familiar with that area of law, it is easy to complicate the problem and go beyond the client's needs from their instructions. This can lead to losing time in an assessment and relying on irrelevant sources, which will impact your ability to apply the law correctly to the client's situation.

You will demonstrate **competence** if you are able to select relevant information to the legal problem and use that information to support your answer. The information should be from a selection of primary and secondary sources.

You will **not** demonstrate **competence** if you do any of the following:
a. You select only irrelevant information.

   Make sure you focus on the client's problem and their goals. This will help you to avoid including irrelevant information. If you are struggling to establish whether the information is relevant, ask yourself: does this source assist me to answer my client's legal question?
b. You do not select enough relevant information.

   You will be given approximately eight sources in the assessment. Not all of them will be relevant. Make sure you consider all the sources given but discuss only the most relevant. You should not rely on only one source.
c. You are unable to distinguish between relevant and irrelevant information.

   If you find it difficult to identify which sources are relevant, it might be tempting to discuss them all. But you are cautioned against this: the SRA states that if your answer contains information from all the sources, regardless of relevance, this demonstrates an inability to identify and use only relevant sources. This means you are not demonstrating the required level of competency.

d. You do not include your legal findings to support your answer in the research note to the partner.

> The partner has specifically asked you to include your legal reasoning, so make sure you do not miss this step.

2. Provide client-focused advice that addresses the client's problem

Try to remain focused on what the client's issue is and what advice they are seeking. It is important to demonstrate that you understand the issue from the client's perspective. Avoid providing generic advice that has minimal relevance to the client's situation.

You will demonstrate **competence** if you can demonstrate an understanding of the client's problem from their perspective. You need to address:
* any relevant commercial considerations
* the client's personal circumstances, priorities, objectives and constraints.

You will **not** demonstrate **competence** if you do not appreciate the client's problem from the client's perspective or do not focus on the issues identified by the client. It will be evident from your research note if you have not considered the client's goals (including the priority of those goals) and any limitations the client may be experiencing, such as monetary limitations and/or time constraints. If the advice you have given is inappropriate, you will not be competent.

3. Use clear, precise, concise and acceptable language

For a reminder of what clear, precise, concise and acceptable language means, please see Chapter 1, page 5.

Assessment technique

Legal research differs from the other SQE2 written assessments because you are expected to use legal terminology, which would be considered jargon by the client. The SRA has provided guidance that the reader of your research note will be a partner in a law firm. Thus, it will be appropriate for you to include specific reference to primary and secondary resources, including precise references to relevant legislation and case law.

You will demonstrate **competence** if you use understandable language that precisely outlines the facts and important information. You also need to use correct legal terminology.

You will **not** demonstrate **competence** if:
* the reader would find it difficult to understand your use of language, because your answer lacks clarity or is poorly expressed
* the reader's understanding would be adversely affected by the density, length or brevity of the answer
* your research note uses unnecessary legal terminology or jargon that is not relevant to the issue you have been asked to research.

APPLICATION OF LAW ASSESSMENT CRITERIA

4. Apply the law correctly to the client's situation

Your FLK is particularly important for your legal research assessment. You will navigate through the sources far more successfully if you have remembered the legal principles you learned for the SQE1 examinations. Remember, if you have any gaps in your knowledge, the *Revise SQE* revision guides cover all subject areas for SQE1: details of all titles are available at revise4law.co.uk.

The SRA has produced a list of legal content on which they might examine you in the SQE2 assessments. You will find this information on the SRA website: https://sqe.sra.org /uk/exam-arrangements/assessment-information. We recommend that you familiarise yourself with those topics.

SRA Code of Conduct for Firms

Make sure you bear in mind the SRA Code of Conduct for Firms. This Code sets out the standards and business controls expected by firms that have been authorised by the SRA to provide legal services.

The Code of Conduct is integral to maintaining the culture and environment for the delivery of legal services to clients.

The SRA Code of Conduct for Firms includes the following paragraphs:

1	Maintaining trust and acting fairly
2	Compliance and business systems
3	Cooperation and accountability
4	Service and competence
5	Client money and assets
6.1–6.2	Conflict of interests
6.3–6.5	Confidentiality and disclosure
7	Applicable standards in the SRA Code of Conduct for Solicitors, RELs and RFLs
8	Managers in SRA authorised firms
9	Compliance officers.

You will demonstrate **competence** if you can:
- identify the relevant fundamental legal principles
- apply them correctly.

You will **not** demonstrate **competence** if you do not identify the relevant legal principles and correctly apply those legal principles to the client's case in a way that addresses the client's needs and concerns.

5. Apply the law comprehensively to the client's situation

You need to identify any ethical and professional conduct issues and exercise judgement to resolve them honestly and with integrity.

You will demonstrate **competence** if your legal analysis is 'sufficiently detailed' in the context of the client's case. For your work to be sufficiently detailed, you need to demonstrate that you can:
- evaluate relevant information to identify key issues and risks
- reach reasonable conclusions in your answer which are supported by evidence
- refer to pertinent ethical issues and/or the SRA Principles and rules of professional conduct.

You will **not** demonstrate **competence** if:
• your analysis is not 'sufficiently detailed' – ie you demonstrate little or no understanding of the key issues and risks
• you fail to apply the law to the facts to reach reasonable conclusions
• you do not consider relevant ethical issues and/or the SRA Principles and rules of professional conduct.

Remember that the question might not ask about specific ethical issues. You will need to recognise these issues independently of the client's question, much the same as you would in legal practice.

◼ A STEPPED APPROACH TO LEGAL RESEARCH

Follow these five basic steps when attempting your legal research assessment:
1. Identify the problem and the client's goal.
2. Identify key words and phrases.
3. Determine a strategy to locate the relevant information.
4. Complete the research.
5. Summarise the advice.

Let us now work through question 1 and break down the steps to complete a legal research assessment. Question 1 focuses on wills and intestacy, probate administration and practice. The stepped approach will assist you to meet the SRA's assessment criteria, which is crucial to success in the assessment.

Remember to review your work in line with the legal research assessment criteria as you complete each step. You can find the criteria on page 34.

◼ QUESTION 1

Email to candidate

From: Partner
Sent: 17 December 202#
To: Candidate
Subject: Ed Walls

Today I met Ed Walls, who is an existing client. Ed is a property developer, and he regularly instructs the firm to carry out conveyancing. The firm has developed a good rapport with him, so I am pleased he has contacted us regarding this new matter.

He is seeking advice regarding the administration of an estate.

Ed was rather distressed during the meeting. His sister and brother-in-law sadly passed away in a car accident, and he is named as the trustee of their estate.

His sister and brother-in-law had both worked very hard during their lifetimes and had accrued a large sum of capital. They also had very good life insurance policies which have paid out a substantial sum into the estate. The beneficiaries of the estate are their two daughters, Sydney and Mia Armstrong. They are both under the age of 18. Ed informed me that the will states his nieces cannot inherit until they turn 25 years of age.

Given that his nieces still have a number of years before they can inherit, Ed feels it would be wise to invest the money as soon as possible.

Ed asked what power he has as a trustee to invest the estate. I have already explained that he has the power to make any kind of investment if he were entitled to the trust subject to the standard investment criteria; that is, there needs to be a diversification of investments of the trust as far as is appropriate, and the suitability of investments must be of the same kind. He seemed to understand this advice well.

Ed then asked what I would recommend he invest in. He is specifically seeking advice on the best shares in the market for investment.

I would like to know whether or not I can give this advice. The firm is not authorised directly by the Financial Conduct Authority.

Please research the answer to this question, using the sources provided, and report back to me so that I can prepare my advice to Ed.

I should like you to include, for my reference, your legal reasoning, mentioning any key sources or authorities.

Many thanks

Partner

Note to candidates:

Given the time constraints of this assessment, we have not provided the full text of some primary sources. For the purposes of this assessment, where the full text of a primary source is not provided, candidates may nevertheless cite the primary source on the basis it is referred to in one or more of the secondary sources provided, and the full text can be checked at a later date.

Information displayed is as obtained on the date of search, for example purposes only. Information contained herein is not to be relied upon outside the purposes of this sample question.

Attachments

You have been provided with the following sources listed alphabetically in order of source name. The order of presentation is not intended as a guide to the order in which they should be consulted.

PLEASE NOTE THAT PART OR ALL OF SOME OF THESE SOURCES MAY NOT BE RELEVANT TO ANSWERING THE QUESTION.

1. *Butler-Sloss & Ors v The Charity Commission for England And Wales & Anor* [2022] EWHC 974 (Ch) (29 April 2022)
2. Financial Services and Markets Act 2000, c 8 ss 19, 22, 23, 26, 325–9, 332
3. Financial Services and Markets Act 2000 (Regulated Activities) Order 2001/544, arts 4, 21, 25, 29, 40, 53, 67, 73, 76, 77
4. *Halsbury's Laws of England*, Financial services regulation, vol. 50, para 271
5. SRA Financial Services (Conduct of Business) Rules
6. SRA Financial Services (Scope) Rules

* * *

Source 1

Contains public sector information licensed under the Open Government Licence v3.0.

Butler-Sloss & Ors v The Charity Commission for England And Wales & Anor [2022] EWHC 974 (Ch) (29 April 2022)

Mr Justice Michael Green:

LAW ON CHARITIES' POWERS OF INVESTMENT

43. Before turning to the *Bishop of Oxford* case, it is important to have in mind some general principles relating to charities and their trustees' powers of investment.
44. Charities can be structured in a number of different ways, including by traditional trust, registered company (normally limited by guarantee), unincorporated association, friendly society and, since January 2013, a Charitable Incorporated Organisation. Both the Ashden and Mark Leonard Trusts are trusts in the strict sense of the word and the Claimants are trustees in the same sense. As such they are subject to the same duties as any other non-charitable trustees. Importantly for these purposes, the Trustee Act 2000 applies to them.
45. In a private trust, the trustees owe their fiduciary and other duties to the beneficiaries who may enforce such duties. Charities have no beneficiaries as such; they are trusts for a public benefit purpose. They are protected and supervised by a combination of the Attorney General, the Charity Commission and the High Court. As Mummery LJ said in *Gaudiya Mission v Brahmachary* [1998] Ch 341, at p.350E:

> 'Under English law charity has always received special treatment. It often takes the form of a trust; but it is a public trust for the promotion of purposes beneficial to the community, not a trust for private individuals. It is therefore subject to special rules governing registration, administration, taxation and duration. Although not a state institution, a charity is subject to the constitutional protection of the Crown as *parens patriae*, acting through the Attorney-General, to the state supervision of the Charity Commissioners and to the judicial supervision of the High Court. This regime applies whether the charity takes the form of a trust or of an incorporated body.'

46. In the recent charity case in the Supreme Court, *Children's Investment Fund (UK) v Attorney General* [2022] AC 155, Lady Arden seems to have concluded that the fiduciary duties owed by trustees (in that case it was actually the member of the incorporated registered charity) are owed '*to the charitable purposes or objects of the charity*' (see [50], also [78] and [200]). The overriding duty of charitable trustees is to further the purposes of the charity (see p.1246A of the *Bishop of Oxford* case) and the Attorney General represents the Crown as *parens patriae* and can enforce the trustees' duties acting in the public interest in ensuring that charities are properly administered.
47. I have set out above the express powers of investment contained in the respective Trust Deeds. The general power of investment set out in the Trustee Act 2000 is also applicable to these trustees. Section 3 of the Trustee Act 2000 defines the general power of investment in the following terms: '*Subject to the provisions of this Part, a trustee may make any kind of investment that he could make if he were absolutely entitled to the assets of the trust.*'
48. The standard investment criteria that must be considered by trustees in exercising their power of investment are set out in s.4 of the Trustee Act 2000 as follows:

> '4. Standard investment criteria
>
> (1) In exercising any power of investment, whether arising under this Part or otherwise, a trustee must have regard to the standard investment criteria.
> (2) A trustee must from time to time review the investments of the trust and consider whether, having regard to the standard investment criteria, they should be varied.
> (3) The standard investment criteria, in relation to a trust, are –
> > (a) the suitability to the trust of investments of the same kind as any particular investment proposed to be made or retained and of that particular investment as an investment of that kind, and
> > (b) the need for diversification of investments of the trust, in so far as is appropriate to the circumstances of the trust.
> (4) This section has effect subject to section 292C(6) of the Charities Act 2011 (which disapplies the duties under this section in cases where they would otherwise apply in relation to a social investment within the meaning of Part 14A of that Act).'

Subsection (4) refers to social investments, which are not relevant to this case. Trustees' duties in relation to social investments are set out in s.292C of the Charities Act 2011.

49. By section 5 of the Trustee Act 2000, before exercising any power of investment, trustees must obtain and consider proper advice about how their power of investment should be exercised. That is subject to the exception in s.5(3) where the trustees have reasonably concluded in all the circumstances that it is unnecessary or inappropriate to obtain such advice. And by s.1 of the Trustee Act 2000, the trustees have a duty of care when exercising their powers of investment.

50. The requirements of the Trustee Act 2000 say nothing about non-financial considerations that can or cannot be taken into account by trustees when exercising their powers of investment. Nor is there anything specific to charities in the Trustee Act 2000, save for the reference to social investments in s.5(5).

51. In relation to social investments, which were introduced into s.292A of the Charities Act 2011 (by the Charities (Protection and Social Investment) Act 2016) these are a hybrid form of investment that charities can make when done '*with a view to both – (a) directly furthering the charity's purposes; and (b) achieving a financial return for the charity*'. This came about because there was uncertainty as to whether charity trustees were able to use their ordinary power of investment when there might be no anticipated positive financial return (see the Law Commission Consultation Paper on *Social Investment by Charities* – Consultation Paper No 216). This case is not about social investments but it is interesting to see why it was thought necessary to provide a specific power to charity trustees to make such investments.

52. In *Cowan v Scargill* [1985] 1 Ch 270, Sir Robert Megarry V-C had to consider whether the trustees of the mineworkers pension scheme, half of whom were appointed by the National Union of Mineworkers, including Mr Arthur Scargill (who represented himself in court), were acting in breach of their duties in blocking an investment plan which included an increase in overseas investment and investments in energy companies that were in direct competition with coal. Such investments would be contrary to the NUM's policy and principles. This was a trust for the provision of financial benefits to individuals, not for a charitable purpose. As such, the Vice-Chancellor held that as this was a trust to provide financial benefits, the power of investment must be exercised to yield the best return for the beneficiaries. However he qualified this moderately by saying that while the trustees' paramount concern must be the beneficiaries' financial benefit, there may be non-financial benefits that the beneficiaries may wish to obtain even if they might as a result receive lesser financial benefits. He thought that this would rarely be the case and it seems to me to be heavily dependent on the fact that the beneficiaries would effectively have to consent to that course

of action. In the case of charities, there are no beneficiaries who can give such consent. That is the situation that the Vice-Chancellor had to contend with in the *Bishop of Oxford* Case, to which I now turn.

*   *   *

Source 2

Financial Services and Markets Act 2000, c 8 ss 19, 22, 23, 26, 325–9, 332

Part 2

19 The general prohibition

(1) No person may carry on a regulated activity in the United Kingdom, or purport to do so, unless he is–
(a) an authorised person; or
(b) an exempt person.
(2) The prohibition is referred to in this Act as the general prohibition.

22 [F1 Regulated activities]

(1) An activity is a regulated activity for the purposes of this Act if it is an activity of a specified kind which is carried on by way of business and—
(a) relates to an investment of a specified kind; or
(b) in the case of an activity of a kind which is also specified for the purposes of this paragraph, is carried on in relation to property of any kind.
[F2(1A) An activity is also a regulated activity for the purposes of this Act if it is an activity of a specified kind which is carried on by way of business and relates to—
(a) information about a person's financial standing, **F3** … **[F4**or]
F5(b) . . . .
[F6(c) administering a benchmark.**]]**
[F7(1B) An activity is also a regulated activity for the purposes of this Act if it is an activity of a specified kind which—
(a) is carried on by way of business in Great Britain, and
(b) is, or relates to, claims management services.]
. . .
(4) 'Investment' includes any asset, right or interest **[F10** (including where an asset, right or interest is, or comprises or represents, a cryptoasset)].
(5) 'Specified' means specified in an order made by the Treasury.

23 Contravention of the general prohibition [F1 or section 20(1) or (1A)]

(1) A person who contravenes the general prohibition is guilty of an offence and liable—
(a) on summary conviction, to imprisonment for a term not exceeding six months or a fine not exceeding the statutory maximum, or both;
(b) on conviction on indictment, to imprisonment for a term not exceeding two years or a fine, or both.

[F2(1A) An authorised person ('A') is guilty of an offence if A carries on a credit-related regulated activity in the United Kingdom, or purports to do so, otherwise than in accordance with permission—
    (a) given to that person under Part 4A, or
    (b) resulting from any other provision of this Act.
(1F) A person guilty of an offence under subsection (1A) is liable—
    (a) on summary conviction, to imprisonment for a term not exceeding the applicable maximum term or a fine not exceeding the statutory maximum, or both;
    (b) on conviction on indictment, to imprisonment for a term not exceeding two years, or a fine, or both.
(1G) The 'applicable maximum term' is—
    (a) in England and Wales **[F3** the general limit in a magistrates' court**]** (or 6 months, if the offence was committed before the commencement of **[F4** 2 May 2022**]**);
    (b) in Scotland, 12 months;
    (c) in Northern Ireland, 6 months.**]**
(2) In this Act 'an authorisation offence' means an offence under this section.
(3) In proceedings for an authorisation offence it is a defence for the accused to show that he took all reasonable precautions and exercised all due diligence to avoid committing the offence.

26 Agreements made by unauthorised persons

(1) An agreement made by a person in the course of carrying on a regulated activity in contravention of the general prohibition is unenforceable against the other party.
(2) The other party is entitled to recover–
    (a) any money or other property paid or transferred by him under the agreement; and
    (b) compensation for any loss sustained by him as a result of having parted with it.
(3) 'Agreement' means an agreement–
    (a) made after this section comes into force; and
    (b) the making or performance of which constitutes, or is part of, the regulated activity in question.
(4) This section does not apply if the regulated activity is accepting deposits.

Part 20

325 **[F1**FCA's**]** general duty

(1) The **[F2**FCA**]** must keep itself informed about–
    (a) the way in which designated professional bodies supervise and regulate the carrying on of exempt regulated activities by members of the professions in relation to which they are established;
    (b) the way in which such members are carrying on exempt regulated activities.
(2) In this Part–
    • 'exempt regulated activities' means regulated activities which may, as a result of this Part, be carried on by members of a profession which is supervised and regulated by a designated professional body without breaching the general prohibition; and
    • 'members', in relation to a profession, means persons who are entitled to practise the profession in question and, in practising it, are subject to the rules of the body designated in relation to that profession, whether or not they are members of that body.
(3) The **[F2**FCA**]** must keep under review the desirability of exercising any of its powers under this Part.

(4) Each designated professional body must co-operate with the **[F2**FCA**]**, by the sharing of information and in other ways, in order to enable the **[F2**FCA**]** to perform its functions under this Part.

326 Designation of professional bodies

(1) The Treasury may by order designate bodies for the purposes of this Part.
(2) A body designated under subsection (1) is referred to in this Part as a designated professional body.
(3) The Treasury may designate a body under subsection (1) only if they are satisfied that–
     (a) the basic condition, and
     (b) one or more of the additional conditions,
     are met in relation to it.
(4) The basic condition is that the body has rules applicable to the carrying on by members of the profession in relation to which it is established of regulated activities which, if the body were to be designated, would be exempt regulated activities.
(5) The additional conditions are that–
     (a) the body has power under any enactment to regulate the practice of the profession;
     (b) being a member of the profession is a requirement under any enactment for the exercise of particular functions or the holding of a particular office;
     (c) the body has been recognised for the purpose of any enactment other than this Act and the recognition has not been withdrawn ...
(6) 'Enactment' includes an Act of the Scottish Parliament, Northern Ireland legislation and subordinate legislation (whether made under an Act, an Act of the Scottish Parliament or Northern Ireland legislation).
(7) 'Recognised' means recognised by–
     (a) a Minister of the Crown;
     (b) the Scottish Ministers;
     (c) a Northern Ireland Minister;
     (d) a Northern Ireland department or its head.

327 Exemption from the general prohibition

(1) The general prohibition does not apply to the carrying on of a regulated activity by a person ('P') if–
     (a) the conditions set out in subsections (2) to (7) are satisfied; **F1** ...
     [F2(aa)where the activity is the provision of a service listed in **[F3**Part 3 of Schedule 2 to the Financial Services and Markets Act 2000 (Regulated Activities) Order 2001]** relating to a financial instrument, the condition set out in subsection (7A) is also satisfied; and**]**
     (b) there is not in force–
          (i)   a direction under section 328, or
          (ii) an order under section 329, which prevents this subsection from applying to the carrying on of that activity by him.
(2) P must be–
     (a) a member of a profession; or
     (b) controlled or managed by one or more such members.
(3) P must not receive from a person other than his client any pecuniary reward or other advantage, for which he does not account to his client, arising out of his carrying on of any of the activities.
(4) The manner of the provision by P of any service in the course of carrying on the activities must be incidental to the provision by him of professional services.

(5) P must not carry on, or hold himself out as carrying on, a regulated activity other than-
  (a) one which rules made as a result of section 332(3) allow him to carry on; or
  (b) one in relation to which he is an exempt person.
(6) The activities must not be of a description, or relate to an investment of a description, specified in an order made by the Treasury for the purposes of this subsection.
(7) The activities must be the only regulated activities carried on by P (other than regulated activities in relation to which he is an exempt person).
[F4 (7A) The condition mentioned in subsection (1)(aa) is that—
  (a) the service is provided in an incidental manner in the course of a professional activity **F5** ...; and
  (b) the professional activity concerned is the provision of professional services.
(7B)   In subsection (7A) a service is provided in an incidental manner in the course of a professional activity **F6** ... if the applicable conditions are satisfied.
(7C)   The applicable conditions for the purposes of subsection (7B) are those set out in **[F7**paragraph 6(a) to (c) of Schedule 3 to the Financial Services and Markets Act 2000 (Regulated Activities) Order 2001**].]**.
(8) 'Professional services' means services-
  (a) which do not constitute carrying on a regulated activity, and
  (b) the provision of which is supervised and regulated by a designated professional body.
[F8 (9) The exemption in this section does not apply to the carrying on of a regulated claims management activity in Great Britain.**]**

328 Directions in relation to the general prohibition

(1) The **[F1FCA]** may direct that section 327(1) is not to apply to the extent specified in the direction.
(2) A direction under subsection (1)-
  (a) must be in writing;
  (b) may be given in relation to different classes of person or different descriptions of regulated activity.
(3) A direction under subsection (1) must be published in the way appearing to the **[F1FCA]** to be best calculated to bring it to the attention of the public.
(4) The **[F1FCA]** may charge a reasonable fee for providing a person with a copy of the direction.
(5) The **[F1FCA]** must, without delay, give the Treasury a copy of any direction which it gives under this section.
[F2 (6) The **[F1FCA]** may exercise the power conferred by subsection (1) only if it is satisfied **F3** ... —
  (a) that it is desirable to do so in order to protect the interests of clients ...**]**
(7) In considering whether it is **[F6**satisfied of the matter specified in subsection (6) (a)**]**, the **[F1FCA]** must have regard amongst other things to the effectiveness of any arrangements made by any designated professional body-
  (a) for securing compliance with rules made under section 332(1);
  (b) for dealing with complaints against its members in relation to the carrying on by them of exempt regulated activities;
  (c) in order to offer redress to clients who suffer, or claim to have suffered, loss as a result of misconduct by its members in their carrying on of exempt regulated activities;
  (d) for co-operating with the [FCA][1] under section 325(4).
(8) In this Part 'clients' means-
  (a) persons who use, have used or are or may be contemplating using, any of the services provided by a member of a profession in the course of carrying on exempt regulated activities;
  (b) persons who have rights or interests which are derived from, or otherwise attributable to, the use of any such services by other persons; or

(c) persons who have rights or interests which may be adversely affected by the use of any such services by persons acting on their behalf or in a fiduciary capacity in relation to them.

(9) If a member of a profession is carrying on an exempt regulated activity in his capacity as a trustee, the persons who are, have been or may be beneficiaries of the trust are to be treated as persons who use, have used or are or may be contemplating using services provided by that person in his carrying on of that activity.

329 Orders in relation to the general prohibition

(1) Subsection (2) applies if it appears to the **[F1** FCA**]** that a person to whom, as a result of section 327(1), the general prohibition does not apply is not a fit and proper person to carry on regulated activities in accordance with that section.

(2) The **[F1** FCA**]** may make an order disapplying section 327(1) in relation to that person to the extent specified in the order.

(3) The **[F1** FCA**]** may, on the application of the person named in an order under subsection (1), vary or revoke it.

(4) 'Specified' means specified in the order.

332 Rules in relation to persons to whom the general prohibition does not apply

(1) The **[F1**FCA**]** may make rules applicable to persons to whom, as a result of section 327(1), the general prohibition does not apply.

(2) The power conferred by subsection (1) is to be exercised for the purpose of ensuring that clients are aware that such persons are not authorised persons.

(3) A designated professional body must make rules–
   (a) applicable to members of the profession in relation to which it is established who are not authorised persons; and
   (b) governing the carrying on by those members of regulated activities (other than regulated activities in relation to which they are exempt persons).

(4) Rules made in compliance with subsection (3) must be designed to secure that, in providing a particular professional service to a particular client, the member carries on only regulated activities which arise out of, or are complementary to, the provision by him of that service to that client.

(5) Rules made by a designated professional body under subsection (3) require the approval of the **[F1**FCA**]**.

*   *   *

Source 3

Contains public sector information licensed under the Open Government Licence v3.0.

Financial Services and Markets Act 2000 (Regulated Activities) Order 2001/544, arts 4, 21, 25, 29, 40, 53, 67, 73, 76, 77

Specified activities: general

4.—(1) The following provisions of this Part specify kinds of activity for the purposes of section 22 of the Act (and accordingly any activity of one of those kinds, which is carried on by way of business[1], and relates to an investment of a kind specified by any provision of Part III and applicable to that activity, is a regulated activity for the purposes of the Act).

(2) The kinds of activity specified by articles 51 and 52 are also specified for the purposes of section 22(1)(b) of the Act (and accordingly any activity of one of those kinds, when carried on by way of business, is a regulated activity when carried on in relation to property of any kind).

(3) Subject to paragraph (4), each provision specifying a kind of activity is subject to the exclusions applicable to that provision (and accordingly any reference in this Order to an activity of the kind specified by a particular provision is to be read subject to any such exclusions).

(4) Where an investment firm—

    (a)   provides core investment services to third parties on a professional basis, and

    (b)   in doing so would be treated as carrying on an activity of a kind specified by a provision of this Part but for an exclusion in any of articles 15, 68, 69 and 70, that exclusion is to be disregarded (and accordingly the investment firm is to be treated as carrying on an activity of the kind specified by the provision in question).

(5) In this article—

"core investment service" means any service listed in section A of the Annex to the investment services directive, the text of which is set out in Schedule 2; and "investment firm" means a person whose regular occupation or business is the provision of core investment services to third parties on a professional basis, other than—

    (a)   a person to whom the investment services directive does not apply by virtue of Article 2.2 of that directive (the text of which is set out in Schedule 3); or

    (b)   a person to whom (if he were incorporated in or formed under the law of an EEA State or, being an individual, had his head office in an EEA State) that directive would not apply by virtue of Article 2.2 of that directive.

---

[1] The Financial Services and Markets Act 2000 (Carrying on Regulated Activities by Way of Business) Order 2001 (S.I. 2001/), made under section 419 of the Act, makes provision as to the circumstances in which persons are, or are not, to be regarded as carrying on activities by way of business.

Dealing in investments as agent

21. Buying, selling, subscribing for or underwriting securities or contractually based investments (other than investments of the kind specified by article 87, or article 89 so far as relevant to that article) as agent is a specified kind of activity.

Arranging deals in investments

25. – (1) Making arrangements for another person (whether as principal or agent) to buy, sell, subscribe for or underwrite a particular investment which is—

    (a) a security,

    (b) a contractually based investment, or

    (c) an investment of the kind specified by article 86, or article 89 so far as relevant to that article, is a specified kind of activity.

(2) Making arrangements with a view to a person who participates in the arrangements buying, selling, subscribing for or underwriting investments falling within paragraph (1)(a), (b) or (c) (whether as principal or agent) is also a specified kind of activity.

Arranging deals with or through authorised persons

29. – (1) There are excluded from article 25(1) and (2) arrangements made by a person ("A") who is not an authorised person for or with a view to a transaction which is or is to be entered into by a person ("the client") with or though an authorised person if—

(a) the transaction is or is to be entered into on advice to the client by an authorised person; or

(b) it is clear, in all the circumstances, that the client, in his capacity as an investor, is not seeking and has not sought advice from A as to the merits of the client's entering into the transaction (or, if the client has sought such advice, A has declined to give it but has recommended that the client seek such advice from an authorised person).

(2) But the exclusion in paragraph (1) does not apply if A receives from any person other than the client any pecuniary reward or other advantage, for which he does not account to the client, arising out of his making the arrangements.

Safeguarding and administering investments

40. –(1) The activity consisting of both—

(a) the safeguarding of assets belonging to another, and

(b) the administration of those assets,

or arranging for one or more other persons to carry on that activity, is a specified kind of activity if the condition in sub-paragraph (a) or (b) of paragraph (2) is met.

(2) The condition is that—

(a) the assets consist of or include any investment which is a security or a contractually based investment; or

(b) the arrangements for their safeguarding and administration are such that the assets may consist of or include such investments, and either the assets have at any time since 1st June 1997 done so, or the arrangements have at any time (whether before or after that date) been held out as ones under which such investments would be safeguarded and administered.

(3) For the purposes of this article—

(a) it is immaterial that title to the assets safeguarded and administered is held in uncertificated form;

(b) it is immaterial that the assets safeguarded and administered may be transferred to another person, subject to a commitment by the person safeguarding and administering them, or arranging for their safeguarding and administration, that they will be replaced by equivalent assets at some future date or when so requested by the person to whom they belong.

Advising on investments

53. Advising a person is a specified kind of activity if the advice is—

(a) given to the person in his capacity as an investor or potential investor, or in his capacity as agent for an investor or a potential investor; and

(b) advice on the merits of his doing any of the following (whether as principal or agent)—

  (i) buying, selling, subscribing for or underwriting a particular investment which is a security or a contractually based investment, or

  (ii) exercising any right conferred by such an investment to buy, sell, subscribe for or underwrite such an investment.

Activities carried on in the course of a profession or non-investment business

67. –(1) There is excluded from articles 21, 25(1) and (2), 40 and 53 any activity which—

(a) is carried on in the course of carrying on any profession or business which does not otherwise consist of regulated activities; and

(b) may reasonably be regarded as a necessary part of other services provided in the course of that profession or business.

(2) But the exclusion in paragraph (1) does not apply if the activity in question is remunerated separately from the other services.

Investments: general

73. The following kinds of investment are specified for the purposes of section 22 of the Act.

Shares etc.

76.—(1) Shares or stock in the share capital of—
  (a) any body corporate (wherever incorporated), and
  (b) any unincorporated body constituted under the law of a country or territory outside the United Kingdom.
(2) Paragraph (1) includes—
  (a) any shares of a class defined as deferred shares for the purposes of section 119 of the Building Societies Act 1986[1]; and
  (b) any transferable shares in a body incorporated under the law of, or any part of, the United Kingdom relating to industrial and provident societies or credit unions, or in a body constituted under the law of another EEA State for purposes equivalent to those of such a body.
(3) But subject to paragraph (2) there are excluded from paragraph (1) shares or stock in the share capital of—
  (a) an open-ended investment company;
  (b) a building society incorporated under the law of, or any part of, the United Kingdom;
  (c) a body incorporated under the law of, or any part of, the United Kingdom relating to industrial and provident societies or credit unions;
  (d) any body constituted under the law of an EEA State for purposes equivalent to those of a body falling within sub-paragraph (b) or (c).

---

[1] 1986 c. 53.

Instruments creating or acknowledging indebtedness

77.—(1) Subject to paragraph (2), such of the following as do not fall within article 78—
  (a) debentures;
  (b) debenture stock;
  (c) loan stock;
  (d) bonds;
  (e) certificates of deposit;
  (f) any other instrument creating or acknowledging indebtedness.
(2) If and to the extent that they would otherwise fall within paragraph (1), there are excluded from that paragraph—
  (a) an instrument acknowledging or creating indebtedness for, or for money borrowed to defray, the consideration payable under a contract for the supply of goods or services;
  (b) a cheque or other bill of exchange, a banker's draft or a letter of credit (but not a bill of exchange accepted by a banker);
  (c) a banknote, a statement showing a balance on a current, deposit or savings account, a lease or other disposition of property, or a heritable security; and
  (d) a contract of insurance.
(3) An instrument excluded from paragraph (1) of article 78 by paragraph (2)(b) of that article is not thereby to be taken to fall within paragraph (1) of this article.

*   *   *

Source 4

Reproduced by permission of RELX (UK) Limited, trading as LexisNexis.

Halsbury's Laws of England > Financial services regulation (Volume 50 (2022), paras 1–589; Volume 50A (2022), paras 590–1072) > 3. Regulated activities > (2) Regulated activities > (iv) Specified investments

(iv) Specified investments

271 Specified kinds of investment

The following kinds of investment are specified investments[1]:
 (1) a deposit ...;
 (2) electronic money ...;
 (3) rights under a contract of insurance ...;
 (4) shares or stock in the share capital of any body corporate (wherever incorporated), and any unincorporated body constituted under the law of a country or territory outside the United Kingdom[5];
 (5) certain: (a) debentures; (b) debenture stock; (c) loan stock; (d) bonds; (e) certificates of deposit; and (f) other instruments creating or acknowledging indebtedness ...;
 (6) certain rights under an alternative finance investment bond[7];
 (7) loan stock, bonds and other instruments creating or acknowledging indebtedness, issued by or on behalf of any of the following: (a) the government of the United Kingdom; (b) the Scottish Administration; (c) the Executive Committee of the Northern Ireland Assembly; (d) Senedd Cymru; (e) the government of any country or territory outside the United Kingdom; (f) a local authority in the United Kingdom or elsewhere; or (g) a body the members of which comprise states including the United Kingdom, or bodies whose members comprise states including the United Kingdom[8];
 (8) warrants and other instruments entitling the holder to subscribe for any investment specified in heads (4) to (7)[9];
 (9) certificates or other instruments which confer contractual or property rights (other than rights consisting of options[10]): (a) in respect of any shares or stock, certain instruments creating or acknowledging indebtedness, government and public securities and instruments giving entitlements to investments, being an investment held by a person other than the person on whom the rights are conferred by the certificate or instrument; and (b) the transfer of which may be effected without the consent of that person ...;
 (10) units in a collective investment scheme ... ;
 (11) rights under a stakeholder pension scheme, rights under a personal pension scheme, and rights or interest under a pension scheme which provides safeguarded benefits ...;

---

[1] Ie they are specified investments for the purposes of the Financial Services and Markets Act 2000 s 22 (see PARA 108): see the Financial Services and Markets Act 2000 (Regulated Activities) Order 2001, SI 2001/544, art 73.

[5] Financial Services and Markets Act 2000 (Regulated Activities) Order 2001, SI 2001/544, art 76(1)(a), (b). This includes any shares of a class defined as deferred shares for the purposes of the Building Societies Act 1986 s 119 (see FINANCIAL INSTITUTIONS VOL 48 (2021) PARA 318) or the Credit Unions Act 1979 s 31A (see FINANCIAL INSTITUTIONS VOL 48 (2021) PARA 924) and any transferable

shares in a body incorporated under the law of, or any part of, the United Kingdom relating to co-operative and community benefit societies, industrial and provident societies or credit unions, or in a body constituted under the law of another EEA state for the purposes equivalent to those of such a body: Financial Services and Markets Act 2000 (Regulated Activities) Order 2001, SI 2001/544, art 76(2) (amended by SI 2011/2687 and SI 2014/1815). However it does not include shares or stock in the share capital of: (1) an open-ended investment company; (2) a building society incorporated under the law of, or any part of, the United Kingdom; (3) a body incorporated under the law of, or any part of, the United Kingdom relating to industrial and provident societies or credit unions: Financial Services and Markets Act 2000 (Regulated Activities) Order 2001, SI 2001/544, art 76(3) (amended by SI 2014/1815). As to the meaning of 'United Kingdom' see PARA 2. As to co-operative and community benefit societies ad industrial and provident societies see **FINANCIAL INSTITUTIONS** VOL 48 (2021) **PARA** 865 et seq. As to the old definition of 'shares' (apparently extending to stock) see *Borland's Trustee v Steel Bros & Co Ltd [1901] 1 Ch 279* at 288.

[7] Financial Services and Markets Act 2000 (Regulated Activities) Order 2001, SI 2001/544, art 77A(1) (art 77A added by SI 2010/86).

This only applies to such rights as do not fall within the Financial Services and Markets Act 2000 (Regulated Activities) Order 2001, SI 2001/544, art 77 or art 78: art 77(1) (amended by SI 2011/133).

[8] Financial Services and Markets Act 2000 (Regulated Activities) Order 2001, SI 2001/544, art 78(1)(a)–(g) (amended by SI 2019/632). This does not include: (1) so far as applicable, the instruments mentioned in the Financial Services and Markets Act 2000 (Regulated Activities) Order 2001, SI 2001/544, arts 77(2)(a)–(d); and (2) any instrument creating or acknowledging indebtedness in respect of: (a) money received by the Director of Savings as deposits or otherwise in connection with the business of the National Savings Bank; or (b) money raised under the National Loans Act 1968 under the auspices of the Director of Savings or treated as so raised by virtue of the National Debt Act 1972 s 11(3) (see **FINANCIAL INSTRUMENTS AND TRANSACTIONS** VOL 49 (2021) **PARA** 108): Financial Services and Markets Act 2000 (Regulated Activities) Order 2001, SI 2001/544, art 78(2) (amended by SI 2010/86).

Head (1) does not exclude an instrument which meets the requirements set out in art 77A(2)(a)–(e): art 78(3) (added by SI 2010/86).

Note that an instrument excluded from art 78(1) by art 78(2)(b) is not thereby to be taken to fall within art 77(1): art 77(3). As to Senedd Cymru see **CONSTITUTIONAL AND ADMINISTRATIVE LAW** VOL 20 (2023) **PARA** 79 et seq.

[9] Financial Services and Markets Act 2000 (Regulated Activities) Order 2001, SI 2001/544, art 79(1) (amended by SI 2010/86). It is immaterial whether the investment to which the entitlement relates is in existence or identifiable: art 79(2). Note that an investment of the kind specified by head (8) in the text is not to be regarded as falling within art 83, art 84 or art 85: art 79(3).

[10] Ie an investment of the kind specified by Financial Services and Markets Act 2000 (Regulated Activities) Order 2001, SI 2001/544, art 83.

* * *

Source 5

This work is owned by and published under licence from the Solicitors Regulation Authority of The Cube, 199 Wharfside Street, Birmingham, B1 1RN, which asserts its right to be identified as the author of this work in accordance with the Copyright, Designs and Patents Act 1988 Sections 77 and 78: www.sra.org.uk/solicitors /standards-regulations/financial-services-conduct-business-rules/. Please refer to the SRA website to ensure you are relying upon the correct version and most up to date version of the Standards.

SRA Financial Services (Conduct of Business) Rules

Part 1: Application

Rule 1: Application

1.1 Apart from rule 2 (Status Disclosure), these rules apply to:
   a) authorised bodies which are not regulated by the FCA;
   b) authorised bodies which are regulated by the FCA, but only in respect of their non-mainstream regulated activities; and
   c) the managers and employees of authorised bodies in (a) and (b) above, and references to 'you' in these rules should be read accordingly.
1.2 Where an authorised body is a licensed body, these rules apply only in relation to the activities regulated by the SRA in accordance with the terms of the body's licence.
1.3 Rule 2 applies only to authorised bodies which are not regulated by the FCA.

Part 2: Rules

Rule 2: Status disclosure

2.1 Notwithstanding the wider information obligations in the SRA Codes of Conduct, you must give the client the following information in writing in a manner that is clear, fair and not misleading before providing a service which includes the carrying on of a regulated financial services activity and in good time before the conclusion of a contract of insurance:
   a) a statement that you are not authorised by the FCA;
   b) your name and practising address;
   c) the nature of the regulated financial services activities carried on by you, and the fact that they are limited in scope;
   d) a statement that you are authorised and regulated by the SRA; and
   e) a statement explaining that complaints and redress mechanisms are provided through the SRA and the Legal Ombudsman.
2.2 Before you provide a service, which includes the carrying on of an insurance distribution activity with or for a client and in good time before the conclusion of a contract of insurance, you must state that you are an ancillary insurance intermediary and make the following statement in writing to the client in a way that is clear, fair and not misleading:

> '[This firm is]/[We are] not authorised by the Financial Conduct Authority. However, we are included on the register maintained by the Financial Conduct Authority so that we can carry on insurance distribution activity, which is broadly the advising on, selling and administration of insurance contracts. This part of our business, including arrangements for complaints or redress if something goes wrong, is regulated by the Solicitors Regulation Authority. The register can be accessed via the Financial Conduct Authority website at www.fca.org.uk/firms/financial-services-register.'

Rule 3: Execution of transactions

3.1 You must ensure that where you have agreed or decided in your discretion to effect a transaction, you must do so as soon as possible, unless you reasonably believe that it is in the client's best interests not to.

Rule 4: Records of transactions

4.1 Where you receive instructions from a client to effect a transaction, or make a decision to effect a transaction in your discretion, you must keep a record of:
  a) the name of the client;
  b) the terms of the instructions or decision; and
  c) in the case of instructions, the date on which they were received.
4.2 Where you give instructions to another person to effect a transaction, you must keep a record of:
  a) the name of the client;
  b) the terms of the instructions;
  c) the date on which the instructions were given; and
  d) the name of the other person instructed.

Rule 5: Record of commissions

5.1 Where you receive commission which is attributable to your regulated financial services activities, you must keep a record of:
  a) the amount of the commission; and
  b) how you have accounted to the client.

Rule 6: Safekeeping of clients' investments

6.1 Where you undertake the regulated financial services activity of safeguarding and administering investments, you must operate appropriate systems, including the keeping of appropriate records, which provide for the safekeeping of assets entrusted to you by clients and others.
6.2 Where such assets are passed to a third party:
  a) you should obtain an acknowledgement of receipt of the property; and
  b) if they have been passed to a third party on the client's instructions, you should obtain such instructions in writing.

Rule 7: Execution-only business

7.1 If you arrange for a client on an execution-only basis any transaction involving a retail investment product, you must send the client written confirmation to the effect that:
  a) the client had not sought and was not given any advice from you in connection with the transaction; or
  b) the client was given advice from you in connection with that transaction but nevertheless persisted in wishing the transaction to be effected,
  and in either case the transaction is effected on the client's explicit instructions.

Rule 8: Retention of records

8.1 Each record which is made under these rules shall be kept for at least six years from the date it is made.

* * *

Source 6

This work is owned by and published under licence from the Solicitors Regulation Authority of The Cube, 199 Wharfside Street, Birmingham, B1 1RN, which asserts its right to be identified as the author of this work in accordance with the Copyright, Designs and Patents Act 1988 Sections 77 and 78: www.sra.org.uk/solicitors /standards-regulations/financial-services-scope-rules/. Please refer to the SRA website to ensure you are relying upon the correct version and most up to date version of the Standards.

SRA Financial Services (Scope) Rules

Rule 1: Application

1.1 These rules apply to authorised bodies that are not regulated by the FCA, their managers and employees and references to 'you' in these rules should be read accordingly.
1.2 Where an authorised body is a licensed body, these rules apply only in relation to the activities regulated by the SRA in accordance with the terms of the body's licence.

Rule 2: Basic conditions

2.1 If you carry on any regulated financial services activities you must ensure that:
    a) you satisfy the conditions in section 327(2) to (5) of FSMA;
    b) the activities arise out of, or are complementary to, the provision of a particular professional service to a particular client;
    c) there is not in force any order or direction of the FCA under sections 328 or 329 of FSMA which prevents you from carrying on the activities; and
    d) the activities are not otherwise prohibited by these rules.

Rule 3: Prohibited activities

3.1 You must not carry on, or agree to carry on, any of the following activities:
    a) an activity that is specified in an order made under section 327(6) of FSMA;
    b) an activity that relates to an investment that is specified in an order made under section 327(6) of FSMA;
    c) entering into a regulated credit agreement as lender except where the regulated credit agreement relates exclusively to the payment of disbursements or professional fees due to you;
    d) exercising, or having the right to exercise, the lender's rights and duties under a regulated credit agreement except where the regulated credit agreement relates exclusively to the payment of disbursements or professional fees due to you;
    e) entering into a regulated consumer hire agreement as owner;
    f) exercising, or having the right to exercise, the owner's rights and duties under a regulated consumer hire agreement;
    g) operating an electronic system in relation to lending within the meaning of article 36H of the Regulated Activities Order;
    h) providing credit references within the meaning of article 89B of the Regulated Activities Order;
    i) insurance distribution activities in relation to insurance-based investment products; or
    j) creating, developing, designing or underwriting a contract of insurance.

Rule 4: Corporate finance

4.1 You must not act as any of the following:
   a) sponsor to an issue in respect of securities to be admitted for dealing on the London Stock Exchange;
   b) nominated adviser to an issue in respect of securities to be admitted for dealing on the Alternative Investment Market of the London Stock Exchange; or
   c) corporate adviser to an issue in respect of securities to be admitted for dealing on the ICAP Securities and Derivatives Exchange or any similar exchange.

Rule 5: Insurance distribution activities

5.1 You may only carry on insurance distribution activities as an ancillary insurance intermediary.
5.2 You must not carry on any insurance distribution activities unless you:
   a) are registered in the Financial Services Register; and
   b) have appointed an insurance distribution officer who will be responsible for your insurance distribution activities.
5.3 If you are carrying on, or proposing to carry on, insurance distribution activities you must notify the SRA in the prescribed form.
5.4 The SRA may give the FCA any of the information collected on the prescribed form and you must notify the SRA without undue delay of any changes to this information or to any information about you that appears on the Financial Services Register.
5.4 Rule 5.3 does not apply to you if you have been registered in the Financial Services Register and are able to carry on insurance mediation activities before 1 October 2018.

Rule 6: Credit-related regulated financial services activities

6.1 You must not enter into any transaction with a client in which you:
   a) provide the client with credit card cheques, a credit or store card, credit tokens, running account credit, a current account or high-cost short-term credit;
   b) hold a continuous payment authority over the client's account; or
   c) take any article from the client in pledge or pawn as security for the transaction.

6.2 You must not:
   a) enter into a regulated credit agreement as lender; or
   b) exercise, or have the right to exercise, the lender's rights and duties under a regulated credit agreement,
   which is secured on land by a legal or equitable mortgage.

6.3 You must not:
   a) enter into a regulated credit agreement as lender; or
   b) exercise, or have the right to exercise, the lender's rights and duties under a regulated credit agreement, which includes a variable rate of interest.

6.4 You must not provide a debt management plan to a client.
6.5 You must not charge a separate fee for, or attribute any element of your fees to, credit broking services.

* * *

STEP 1 IDENTIFY THE PROBLEM AND THE CLIENT'S GOAL

HAVE A GO

Before you can start your research, you need to establish:
* the client's problem – this could be an issue they are experiencing or a general query
* the client's goal.

This will help you determine what you will need to research. Can you list these?

You might have identified the problem as: What investment advice is the law firm allowed to provide for Ed? However, the client's goal is to receive advice on which shares they should invest in. For this assessment, the client's goal and the problem set by the question are not the same. It is important that you consider both, to satisfy the SRA's assessment criteria.

STEP 2 IDENTIFY KEY WORDS AND PHRASES

Once you have identified and summarised the problem and the client's goals, think about the relevant key words and phrases that might assist your research.

In practice you would compile a list of key words and phrases to help you navigate legal search engines, such as Lexis+, Westlaw and Practical Law. Whilst the SQE2 assessment differs from practice because you will be given your research sources, it is still beneficial to identify key words and phrases to sift through those sources, so that you can quickly find the most relevant sources of information. Remember, you do not have a lot of time in this assessment, and you will have many documents to read. As an example, the SRA has published a sample research question on the SRA website which has 30 pages worth of sources.

HAVE A GO

Try to list all of the key words and phrases from the question that might help to guide your research.

Below is our list of key words and phrases for this question:
* investments
* law firms
* trust
* property
* Solicitors Regulation Authority
* stock market
* shares
* regulated activities
* financial services
* professional bodies
* professionals.

During the SQE2 assessment, do not panic if the problem is based on an area of law in which you have gaps in your knowledge. Keep calm and use your key words to find the information you need. Solicitors are constantly learning new law and applying it to their cases, and this is no different from what you are being asked to do in the SQE2 assessment.

STEP 3 DETERMINE A STRATEGY TO LOCATE THE RELEVANT INFORMATION

A helpful way to prepare for the legal research assessment is to develop a strategy for how to assess the different sources in a logical and timely manner.

Your strategy could take various forms, depending on your individual needs and your confidence in that area of law. See the Assessment technique box below for a sample strategy, but remember that you should adjust this strategy to suit your own approach.

Assessment technique

1. Use the list of sources

At the end of the email from the partner, before the sources start, there will be a list of the provided sources to complete your legal research. There should be a mix of primary and secondary sources. The sources are listed alphabetically, but you do not need to consider the sources in that order. In fact, we would discourage this. Instead, use the list of sources to find the secondary sources first.

Secondary sources often provide a commentary on the law, which means the source will be easier to understand quickly and will give you a broad overview to aid your comprehension. Remember about the differences between primary and secondary sources on page 33.

2. Use key words to identify relevant secondary sources

You will be given many different sources in the SQE2 assessment, and not all will be relevant. Once you have identified the problem and the client's goals (**Step 1**) and key words/phrases (**Step 2**), use these key words/phrases to identify which of the secondary sources contain relevant information and which do not. This process of elimination will help you to manage your time effectively.

3. Once you have a basic understanding, review the primary sources

At this stage you will have already identified from the secondary sources what primary sources are relevant. You will often see primary sources referenced in the footnotes. Compare the primary sources referenced in the footnotes with the primary sources in the list. This will help you to manage your time efficiently and quickly identify which source you should read next.

4. Check the law is in force

As you know, the law is constantly evolving. It is therefore crucial that you check the information you are finding is in force. If you are advising a client about law that is no longer in force, this is negligence. The sources provided in the SQE2 assessment are likely to be in force, but keep an eye out for anything in the footnotes that suggests legislation has been repealed.

This part of the strategy links to professional conduct issues. As a solicitor you will need to be competent when carrying out your role, and part of that competency is keeping your professional knowledge and skills up to date (para 4.3 of the SRA Code of Conduct for Firms).

HAVE A GO

Can you apply the steps in this strategy to the facts of question 1?

See below for an example of how to achieve this for question 1.

Example: question 1

1. Use the list of sources

The first step is to identify the type of source by looking through the list:
1. *Butler-Sloss & Ors v The Charity Commission for England And Wales & Anor* [2022] EWHC 974 (Ch) (29 April 2022): **case report – primary source**
2. Financial Services and Markets Act 2000, c 8 ss 19, 22, 23, 26, 325–9, 332: **statute – primary source**
3. Financial Services and Markets Act 2000 (Regulated Activities) Order 2001/544 arts 4, 21, 25, 29, 40, 53, 67, 73, 76, 77: **statutory instrument – primary source**
4. *Halsbury's Laws of England*, Financial services regulation, vol. 50, para 271: **secondary source**
5. SRA Financial Services (Conduct of Business) Rules: **rules – primary source**
6. SRA Financial Services (Scope) Rules: **rules – primary source**.

Only Source 4 is a secondary source. We will therefore focus on this one first.

2. Use key words to identify relevant secondary sources

Source 4 mentions 'financial services regulation', which is closest to our key words and phrases. This is likely to be relevant to our research. We will therefore start by reading Source 4 first.

3. Once you have a basic understanding, review the primary sources

Source 4 repeatedly refers to the Financial Services and Markets Act 2000 (Regulated Activities) Order 2001 and specific sections within that legislation. When we cross-reference that legislation with the list of sources, we note that Source 3 is the Financial Services and Markets Act 2000 (Regulated Activities) Order 2001. We should therefore deduce that this legislation is relevant and review that source next.

4. Check the law is in force

The sources reveal that the Trustee Investments Act 1961 was generally repealed by the Trustee Act 2000. Thus, we should not look at the Trustee Investments Act 1961 and instead focus on the Trustee Act 2000 which is in force.

STEP 4 COMPLETE THE RESEARCH

Assessment technique

In the assessment, you may or may not be provided with the full text of some primary sources. This is due to the limited duration of the exam. Where the full text of a primary source is not provided, you should still cite the relevant primary source on the basis it is referred to in one or more of the secondary sources provided, and the full text can be checked at a later date.

HAVE A GO

Using the strategy in **Step 3**, you should be able to complete the research for question 1.

Remember that you do not need to make a record of your research trail. Instead, focus on making notes of the answers you find.

Assessment technique

Note that you are not able to highlight information in the SQE2 assessments. If you want to use the copy and paste function when eliciting legal reasoning to save time, make sure you use CTRL+C on your keyboard to copy and CTRL+V to paste.

The example box below sets out which sources are relevant or irrelevant to the issues being researched.

Example: question 1

Relevant sources:

2. Financial Services and Markets Act 2000, c 8 ss 19, 22, 23, 26, 325–9, 332: **primary source**
3. Financial Services and Markets Act 2000 (Regulated Activities) Order 2001/544 arts 4, 21, 25, 29, 40, 53, 67, 73, 76, 77: **primary source**
4. *Halsbury's Laws of England*, Financial services regulation, vol. 50, para 271: **secondary source**
6. SRA Financial Services (Scope) Rules: **primary source**.

Irrelevant sources:

1. *Butler-Sloss & Ors v The Charity Commission for England And Wales & Anor* [2022] EWHC 974 (Ch) (29 April 2022): **primary source**
5. SRA Financial Services (Conduct of Business) Rules: **primary source**.

➡Key legal points: question 1

Your FLK from SQE1 should lead you to make the following legal points from your research:

The SRA requires all providers of legal services to understand what financial advice they may or may not offer to their clients.

Law firms and individuals must be able to advise their clients on how certain transactions may be regulated by the Financial Services and Markets Act 2000.

There is a general prohibition under s 19(1) of the Financial Services and Markets Act 2000 which states that no person may carry on a regulated activity in the United Kingdom or purport to do so unless he is –
(a) an authorised person; or
(b) an exempt person.

We will explore what each of these points mean in the sample answers to this question.

SQE 1 Functioning legal knowledge link

You will navigate through the sources far more successfully if you can remember the legal principles that you learned for your SQE1 examinations. You can find the legislation in Source 2 on pages 41–45. See *Revise SQE: Business Law and Practice* to refresh your FLK for this area of law.

STEP 5 WRITE YOUR ANSWER

Once you have completed the research, you are ready to make notes which will be the basis of your advice. Your research note should confirm what advice to give to the client and the legal reasoning including any key sources or authorities. In the SQE2 assessment you will be provided with an answer template for your research note, which is an email to a partner.

HAVE A GO

The structure of your research note could take various forms, depending upon your individual needs and your confidence in that legal area. The Assessment technique box below offers a structure we recommend you follow, but bear in mind that this is only an example, and you can adjust this strategy to suit you. If you have prepared a structure in advance, you are more likely to be successful in the assessment.

Assessment technique

You should include the following elements in your research note.

1. **Background**

   This part of the research note should include an outline of the facts/client's instructions. It is difficult to demonstrate an application of law if you do not include the facts to which the law is being applied.

2. **What you have researched**

   Explain what you have researched. You could also discuss here what the client's goal is, if appropriate.

3. **Advice and legal reasoning**

   Then answer the question.
   - Your explanation must use clear, precise and concise appropriate language for addressing the reader (for this assessment, a partner in a law firm).
   - Include only the most relevant and accurate law.
   - Discuss all the relevant principles that you have considered from your legal research.
   - Your answer could be a mixture of quoting legislation from statute sources and providing a summary of key principles.
   - You can copy and paste *extracts* of the sources into your report, but do not copy and paste an entire source.
   - When you copy and paste legislation, you must explain its relevance to the question, as evidence of your ability to apply the law.

4. **Conclusion/Next steps**

   Discuss any next steps, if relevant to the scenario. For example, there might be missing information which you will need to obtain from the client.

   While you draft your answer, you could use these headings to help with the structure. You can then remove them on a final readthrough.

■ YOUR TURN

Now that we have talked through the steps of legal research, have a go at completing a research note to the partner in question 1.
- Make sure that you address each point in the assessment criteria (see page 34).
- Use the five steps on page 37 as a method for approaching the assessment.
- Structure your answer around the headings suggested on page 59, but remember to remove the headings at the end of the assessment.
- Do not forget to time yourself. Timings are important: you will need to prepare and write your answer in 60 minutes.

EVALUATING YOUR ANSWER

Once you have attempted completing the report, mark it yourself against the SQE2 legal research assessment criteria. Do you think your attempt met the threshold standard?

Now compare your attempt against the two sample answers below. A circled number indicates that commentary is provided for this part of the answer. The commentary will explain whether or not the sample is likely to meet the SQE2 standard threshold.

■ SAMPLE ANSWER 1 TO QUESTION 1

Ed Walls is the trustee of his sister and brother-in-law's estate. They have passed away. The beneficiaries of the estate are his two nieces, Sydney and Mia Armstrong, who are under the age of 18. The beneficiaries will inherit when they reach 25 years.

Ed is seeking advice on what shares in the market he should invest the trust in. The firm is not directly authorised by the Financial Conduct Authority to give investment advice and I have researched whether or not the firm can give advice on what specific shares he should invest in. **❶**

I have concluded that we cannot give him advice on what specific shares he should invest in. **❷**

Section 19(1) of the Financial Services and Markets Act 2000 states that no person may carry on a regulated activity in the United Kingdom, or purport to do so, unless he is (a) an authorised person; or (b) an exempt person.

Regulated activity is defined by s 22(1) of the Financial Services and Markets Act 2000 as an activity of a specified kind which is carried on in the way of business and relates to an investment of a specified kind.

Article 53 Financial Services and Markets Act 2000 (Regulated Activities) Order 2001/544 specifies that advising on investments is a specified kind of activity. *Halsbury's Laws of England*, Financial services regulation, vol. 50, para 271 outlines that investment in shares is a specified investment. Article 76 Financial Services and Markets Act 2000 (Regulated Activities) Order 2001/544 states that advice specifically on shares is an investment of a specified kind. This means that advice on shares investment is an activity of a specified kind, which is a regulated activity. Thus, if the firm gave advice to Ed on shares investment, the firm would be carrying out a regulated activity under s 19(1) of the Financial Services and Markets Act 2000. **❸**

The advice is being sought in the law firm's capacity as a business. Article 67 Financial Services and Markets Act 2000 (Regulated Activities) Order 2001/544 states we can only give advice of this nature where the advice is necessary.

As you mentioned in your email, the firm is not authorised to give advice, which is set out under s 19(1) of the Financial Services and Markets Act 2000. ❹

The firm will only be exempt if we satisfy the conditions under s 327 Financial Services and Markets Act 2000, and the SRA Financial Services (Scope) Rules.

The conditions set out in s 327 Financial Services and Markets Act 2000 include:
- (2) P must be–
    - (a) a member of a profession; or
    - (b) controlled or managed by one or more such members.
- (3) P must not receive from a person other than his client any pecuniary reward or other advantage, for which he does not account to his client, arising out of his carrying on of any of the activities.
- (4) The manner of the provision by P of any service in the course of carrying on the activities must be incidental to the provision by him of professional services.
- (5) P must not carry on, or hold himself out as carrying on, a regulated activity other than–
    - (a) one which rules made as a result of section 332(3) allow him to carry on; or
    - (b) one in relation to which he is an exempt person.

Section 332(3) Financial Services and Markets Act 2000 states 'a designated professional body must make rules– (a) applicable to members of the profession in relation to which it is established who are not authorised persons; and (b) governing the carrying on by those members of regulated activities (other than regulated activities in relation to which they are exempt persons)'.

The designated professional body for solicitors is the SRA, and law firms must therefore comply with the SRA Financial Services (Scope) Rules and the SRA Financial Services (Conduct of Business) Rules. ❺

Rule 2.1 SRA Financial Services (Scope) Rules states that if you carry on any regulated financial services activities which is defined to mean an activity which is specified in the Financial Services and Markets Act 2000 (Regulated Activities) Order 2001, you must ensure that you satisfy the conditions in s 327(2) to (5) of FSMA (Financial Services and Markets Act); the activities arise out of, or are complementary to, the provision of a particular professional service to a particular client; there is not in force any order or direction of the FCA under ss 328 or 329 of FSMA which prevents you from carrying on the activities; and the activities are not otherwise prohibited by these rules.

The firm is therefore not exempt under s 19(1) of the Financial Services and Markets Act 2000 because the advice Ed is requesting goes beyond necessary or generic advice. What the firm is being asked to advise on is not complementary to or incidental to the provision of a conveyancing service which we are offering to Ed. ❻

The next step would be to refer Ed to an independent financial advisor, an authorised person who can give this advice. ❼

COMMENTARY

1 These opening paragraphs are client-focused, and address the issue being researched as well as the factual background.

2 This paragraph states the answer to the research posed. The language used is clear, precise and concise as per the assessment criteria. The partner at the firm is looking for a summary of the advice which is easy to understand and can be thereafter passed on to the client.

3 Whilst a lot of legal reasoning could be referred to, s 19(1) of the Financial Services and Markets Act 2000 is the most crucial for the partner to be made aware of. Remember that s 19(1) contains the legal requirements that must be met for advice to be given to Ed in this context. By identifying this source, the candidate demonstrates an ability to identify and use relevant sources.

4 Remember that this research note is intended to be used as the basis of a legal letter to Ed. Therefore, the candidate rightly includes enough information for the partner to understand why the firm cannot give this advice to Ed.

5 The candidate rightly identifies the relevant professional body and therefore applies the source correctly.

6 This paragraph demonstrates an application of the law to the client's facts. Ed is an existing conveyancing client, and advice on shares investments is not incidental to the provision of a conveyancing service. Therefore, the advice is not exempt.

7 This paragraph includes a relevant next step for the client. Whilst the firm would be breaching legislation and professional conduct if they provided the advice, there are other individuals such as independent financial advisors who can give this advice. The candidate therefore exercises their judgement to resolve the client's issue with honesty and integrity (assessment criterion 5) by suggesting a referral is made to an appropriate person, therefore meeting the client's goal.

Does this answer meet the threshold?

The sample answer reaches the correct conclusion, which is that the law firm cannot give advice on shares investments. The candidate has correctly identified first that Sources 1 and 6 are not relevant, and second why the firm cannot give advice on share investments – because the firm is neither authorised nor exempt. The sample answer has applied the law comprehensively to the client's situation and identified professional conduct issues for the law firm. A next step has been given, which demonstrates an attempt to resolve the issue for the client with honesty and integrity. Relevant sources have been selected and applied to the facts to provide reasonable advice to the client. It is therefore likely that this sample answer would meet the threshold standard for the SQE2 legal research assessment.

Now let's consider the second sample answer to question 1.

■ SAMPLE ANSWER 2 TO QUESTION 1

We might be able to advise Ed on shares generally. **1**

If we advise Ed on which shares, he should invest in in on the current market we will most likely be breaching the rules under Financial Services and Markets Act 2000. There will be consequences for breaching this legislation. The consequences are sever, probably not worth our practicing certificates. **2**

The consequences include:

23 Contravention of the general prohibition [F1 or section 20(1) or (1A)]

(1) A person who contravenes the general prohibition is guilty of an offence and liable—
   (a) on summary conviction, to imprisonment for a term not exceeding six months or a fine not exceeding the statutory maximum, or both;
   (b) on conviction on indictment, to imprisonment for a term not exceeding two years or a fine, or both.

[F2(1A) An authorised person ('A') is guilty of an offence if A carries on a credit-related regulated activity in the United Kingdom, or purports to do so, otherwise than in accordance with permission—
   (a) given to that person under Part 4A, or
   (b) resulting from any other provision of this Act.

(1F) A person guilty of an offence under subsection (1A) is liable—
   (a) on summary conviction, to imprisonment for a term not exceeding the applicable maximum term or a fine not exceeding the statutory maximum, or both;
   (b) on conviction on indictment, to imprisonment for a term not exceeding two years, or a fine, or both.

(1G) The 'applicable maximum term' is—
   (a) in England and Wales, [F3 the general limit in a magistrates' court] (or 6 months, if the offence was committed before the commencement of [F4 2 May 2022]);
   (b) in Scotland, 12 months;
   (c) in Northern Ireland, 6 months. ③

26 Agreements made by unauthorised persons

(1) An agreement made by a person in the course of carrying on a regulated activity in contravention of the general prohibition is unenforceable against the other party.

(2) The other party is entitled to recover–
   (a) any money or other property paid or transferred by him under the agreement; and
   (b) compensation for any loss sustained by him as a result of having parted with it.

(3) 'Agreement' means an agreement–
   (a) made after this section comes into force; and
   (b) the making or performance of which constitutes, or is part of, the regulated activity in question.

(4) This section does not apply if the regulated activity is accepting deposits. ④

Butler-Sloss & Ors v The Charity Commission for England And Wales & Anor [2022] EWHC 974 (Ch) (29 April 2022)

45. In a private trust, the trustees owe their fiduciary and other duties to the beneficiaries who may enforce such duties. Charities have no beneficiaries as such; they are trusts for a public benefit purpose. They are protected and supervised by a combination of the Attorney General, the Charity Commission and the High Court. As Mummery LJ said in *Gaudiya Mission v Brahmachary [1998] Ch 341*, at p.350E ⑤

Financial Services and Markets Act 2000, c 8

Financial Services and Markets Act 2000 (Regulated Activities) Order 2001/544

Halsbury's Laws of England, Financial services regulation, vol. 50, para 271

SRA Financial Services (Conduct of Business) Rules

SRA Financial Services (Scope) Rules ⑥

COMMENTARY

① This sentence is vague and does not answer the question posed. The language is unclear, and the sentence does not give sufficient detail about what the research is focusing on.

② This paragraph is poorly phrased and contains spelling and punctuation errors which the candidate should have picked up when reading through their answer. It is unclear which rules under Financial Services and Markets Act 2000 will be breached. It is not concise, precise or clear, and it is also unprofessional. Remember that emails between colleagues regarding a case should still be placed on that client's file. Clients can request their file and thus see unprofessional emails like this, which would give a bad impression of the firm. The paragraph also uses subjective terminology. Stating that the consequences are sever(e) is incredibly vague and open to interpretation. It is also not clear which rule under the Financial Services and Markets Act 2000 would be breached.

③ Whilst this section sets out one of the consequences of breaching s 19(1) Financial Services and Markets Act 2000, it is not the focus of the research. This is why **Step 1** of our approach to the legal research assessment is important (see page 55). This candidate has also just copied and pasted the legislation, and has not explained the application of the law to the facts of the case.

④ This paragraph has the same weaknesses as above. The law has not been applied to the client's case, and instead the candidate has just copied the source without any analysis or application. There is no evidence that the law has been applied comprehensively to the client's situation. There has been no attempt to resolve the issue with honesty and integrity.

⑤ This paragraph has been copied from Source 1. Regardless of whether or not the content is relevant, it is not appropriate to include this without explanation. In this case, Source 1 is not relevant to the research, so the correct law has not been applied.

⑥ In this part of the answer all the sources have been listed, which is an error we highlighted in **Step 5,** page 59. The candidate does not include any legal reasoning or demonstrate an ability to identify only relevant sources. There has been no attempt to distinguish relevant from irrelevant sources, and the candidate does not specifically refer to relevant sections within the legislation or explain why those sections are relevant.

Does this answer meet the threshold?

It is unlikely that this answer would meet the threshold standard for SQE2 legal research. When compared with the SQE2 legal research assessment criteria, the answer does not apply the relevant law precisely, it is not clear and it has omissions that have affected the advice provided. Whilst the correct consequences of action are listed, this should not have been the primary focus of the legal research and research note. This means that the answer does not meet the client's objective or research the correct question.

Now you can work through question 2, which focuses on business practice in the context of advising and arranging a deal in investments. Make sure that you review your work in line with the SRA's legal research assessment criteria as you complete each step: remember the guidance on pages 34–36.

■ QUESTION 2

Email to candidate

From: Partner
Sent: 18 May 202#
To: Candidate
Subject: IG Ltd

We have been instructed by Jai Rivers on behalf of the company, IG Ltd. This is a private company.

The company wants to purchase buyback shares which are being sold by a shareholder called Katie Roberts. Katie is keen to quickly cash in her shares for her retirement fund. She currently owns 100 shares.

During the meeting yesterday we discussed how the company intended to buy back the shares. Jai hopes to finance the shares from capital. I have advised him that he can only do this when the company has used up distributable profits and the proceeds of any fresh issue of shares made for the purpose of financing the repurchase.

The company has distributable profits of £10,000.

The company has an issued share capital of £50,000 which compromises 50,000 shares of £1. The agreed buyback figure is £25,000. This means that the permissible capital payment will be £15,000.

I advised Jai of the procedural requirements that the company needs to satisfy under the Companies Act 2006, and we discussed the possibility of stamp duty liability. He has instructed us to generate the relevant documents to arrange the buyback, which I agreed to do.

Following the meeting, the firm's managing director, who is a private client specialist, emailed me asking why I have arranged a deal in investments which is a regulated activity. She stated that I should not have given this advice because the firm is neither an authorised nor exempt person. My understanding is that I can give this advice, but I am starting to worry that I have misunderstood the relevant legislation.

Please research the answer to this question, using the sources provided, and report back to me so that I can prepare my response to the managing director.

Please include, for my reference and hers, your legal reasoning, mentioning any key sources or authorities.

Many thanks
Partner

Note to candidates:

Given the time constraints of this assessment, we have not provided the full text of some primary sources. For the purposes of this assessment, where the full text of a primary source is not provided, candidates may nevertheless cite the primary source on the basis it is referred to in one or more of the secondary sources provided, and the full text can be checked at a later date.

Information displayed is as obtained on the date of search, for example purposes only. Information contained herein is not to be relied upon outside the purposes of this sample question.

Attachments

You have been provided with the following sources listed alphabetically in order of source name. The order of presentation is not intended as a guide to the order in which they should be consulted.

PLEASE NOTE THAT PART OR ALL OF SOME OF THESE SOURCES MAY NOT BE RELEVANT TO ANSWERING THE QUESTION.

1. Companies Act 2006, c 46 ss 733, 734
2. Financial Services and Markets Act 2000, c 8 ss 19, 22, 23, 26, 325–9, 332
3. Financial Services and Markets Act 2000 (Regulated Activities) Order 2001/544, arts 4, 21, 25, 29, 40, 53, 67, 73, 76, 77
4. *Halsbury's Laws of England*, Financial Services Regulation, vol. 50 (2022), para 146
5. *Halsbury's Laws of England*, Financial Services Regulation, vol. 50 (2022), para 255
6. The Companies (Model Articles) Regulations 2008, arts 33–5, 75–7

*   *   *

Source 1

Contains public sector information licensed under the Open Government Licence v3.0.

Companies Act 2006, c 46 ss 733, 734

Chapter 7

Supplementary provisions

733 The capital redemption reserve

(1) In the following circumstances a company must transfer amounts to a reserve, called the 'capital redemption reserve'.
(2) Where under this Part shares of a limited company are redeemed or purchased wholly out of the company's profits, the amount by which the company's issued share capital is diminished in accordance with—
   (a) section 688(b) (on the cancellation of shares redeemed), or
   (b) section 706(b)(ii) (on the cancellation of shares purchased),
   must be transferred to the capital redemption reserve.
(3) If—
   (a) the shares are redeemed or purchased wholly or partly out of the proceeds of a fresh issue, and
   (b) the aggregate amount of the proceeds is less than the aggregate nominal value of the shares redeemed or purchased,
   the amount of the difference must be transferred to the capital redemption reserve.

    This does not apply in the case of a private company if, in addition to the proceeds of the fresh issue, the company applies a payment out of capital under Chapter 5 **[F1** or under section 692(1ZA)**]** in making the redemption or purchase.

(4) The amount by which a company's share capital is diminished in accordance with section 729(4) (on the cancellation of shares held as treasury shares) must be transferred to the capital redemption reserve.

(5) The company may use the capital redemption reserve to pay up new shares to be allotted to members as fully paid bonus shares.

(6) Subject to that, the provisions of the Companies Acts relating to the reduction of a company's share capital apply as if the capital redemption reserve were part of its paid up share capital.

734 Accounting consequences of payment out of capital

(1) This section applies where a payment out of capital is made in accordance with Chapter 5 (redemption or purchase of own shares by private company out of capital) **[F2** or section 692(1ZA)**]**.

[F3 (1A) In relation to a payment under section 692(1ZA) references to the permissible capital payment are to the purchase price of the shares or (if less) the part of it met out of the payment under section 692(1ZA) and any proceeds of a fresh issue used to make the purchase.**]**

(2) If the permissible capital payment is less than the nominal amount of the shares redeemed or purchased, the amount of the difference must be transferred to the company's capital redemption reserve.

(3) If the permissible capital payment is greater than the nominal amount of the shares redeemed or purchased—

    (a) the amount of any capital redemption reserve, share premium account or fully paid share capital of the company, and

    (b) any amount representing unrealised profits of the company for the time being standing to the credit of any revaluation reserve maintained by the company,

    may be reduced by a sum not exceeding (or by sums not in total exceeding) the amount by which the permissible capital payment exceeds the nominal amount of the shares.

(4) Where the proceeds of a fresh issue are applied by the company in making a redemption or purchase of its own shares in addition to a payment out of capital under **[F4** Chapter 5**]**, the references in subsections (2) and (3) to the permissible capital payment are to be read as referring to the aggregate of that payment and those proceeds.

*   *   *

Source 2

Financial Services and Markets Act 2000, c 8 ss 19, 22, 23, 26, 325–9, 332

Part 2

19 The general prohibition

(1) No person may carry on a regulated activity in the United Kingdom, or purport to do so, unless he is–
  (a) an authorised person; or
  (b) an exempt person.
(2) The prohibition is referred to in this Act as the general prohibition.

22 **[F1 Regulated activities]**

(1) An activity is a regulated activity for the purposes of this Act if it is an activity of a specified kind which is carried on by way of business and—
  (a) relates to an investment of a specified kind; or
  (b) in the case of an activity of a kind which is also specified for the purposes of this paragraph, is carried on in relation to property of any kind.
[F2(1A) An activity is also a regulated activity for the purposes of this Act if it is an activity of a specified kind which is carried on by way of business and relates to—
  (a) information about a person's financial standing, **F3** ... **[F4**or]
  F5(b) . . . .
  [F6(c) administering a benchmark.**]]**
[F7(1B) An activity is also a regulated activity for the purposes of this Act if it is an activity of a specified kind which—
  (a) is carried on by way of business in Great Britain, and
  (b) is, or relates to, claims management services.]
...
(4) 'Investment' includes any asset, right or interest **[F10** (including where an asset, right or interest is, or comprises or represents, a cryptoasset)]**.
(5) 'Specified' means specified in an order made by the Treasury.

23 Contravention of the general prohibition [**F1** or section 20(1) or (1A)]
(1) A person who contravenes the general prohibition is guilty of an offence and liable—
  (a) on summary conviction, to imprisonment for a term not exceeding six months or a fine not exceeding the statutory maximum, or both;
  (b) on conviction on indictment, to imprisonment for a term not exceeding two years or a fine, or both.
[F2(1A) An authorised person ('A') is guilty of an offence if A carries on a credit-related regulated activity in the United Kingdom, or purports to do so, otherwise than in accordance with permission—
  (a) given to that person under Part 4A, or
  (b) resulting from any other provision of this Act.

(1F) A person guilty of an offence under subsection (1A) is liable—
   (a) on summary conviction, to imprisonment for a term not exceeding the applicable maximum term or a fine not exceeding the statutory maximum, or both;
   (b) on conviction on indictment, to imprisonment for a term not exceeding two years, or a fine, or both.
(1G) The 'applicable maximum term' is—
   (a) in England and Wales, **[F3** the general limit in a magistrates' court**]** (or 6 months, if the offence was committed before the commencement of **[F4** 2 May 2022**]**);
   (b) in Scotland, 12 months;
   (c) in Northern Ireland, 6 months.**]**
(2) In this Act 'an authorisation offence' means an offence under this section.
(3) In proceedings for an authorisation offence it is a defence for the accused to show that he took all reasonable precautions and exercised all due diligence to avoid committing the offence.

26 Agreements made by unauthorised persons

(1) An agreement made by a person in the course of carrying on a regulated activity in contravention of the general prohibition is unenforceable against the other party.
(2) The other party is entitled to recover–
   (a) any money or other property paid or transferred by him under the agreement; and
   (b) compensation for any loss sustained by him as a result of having parted with it.
(3) 'Agreement' means an agreement–
   (a) made after this section comes into force; and
   (b) the making or performance of which constitutes, or is part of, the regulated activity in question.
(4) This section does not apply if the regulated activity is accepting deposits.

Part 20

325 **[F1**FCA's**]** general duty

(1) The **[F2**FCA]** must keep itself informed about–
   (a) the way in which designated professional bodies supervise and regulate the carrying on of exempt regulated activities by members of the professions in relation to which they are established;
   (b) the way in which such members are carrying on exempt regulated activities.
(2) In this Part–
   • 'exempt regulated activities' means regulated activities which may, as a result of this Part, be carried on by members of a profession which is supervised and regulated by a designated professional body without breaching the general prohibition; and
   • 'members', in relation to a profession, means persons who are entitled to practise the profession in question and, in practising it, are subject to the rules of the body designated in relation to that profession, whether or not they are members of that body.
(3) The **[F2**FCA]** must keep under review the desirability of exercising any of its powers under this Part.
(4) Each designated professional body must co-operate with the **[F2**FCA]**, by the sharing of information and in other ways, in order to enable the **[F2**FCA]** to perform its functions under this Part.

326 Designation of professional bodies

(1) The Treasury may by order designate bodies for the purposes of this Part.
(2) A body designated under subsection (1) is referred to in this Part as a designated professional body.
(3) The Treasury may designate a body under subsection (1) only if they are satisfied that–
  (a) the basic condition, and
  (b) one or more of the additional conditions,
  are met in relation to it.
(4) The basic condition is that the body has rules applicable to the carrying on by members of the profession in relation to which it is established of regulated activities which, if the body were to be designated, would be exempt regulated activities.
(5) The additional conditions are that–
  (a) the body has power under any enactment to regulate the practice of the profession;
  (b) being a member of the profession is a requirement under any enactment for the exercise of particular functions or the holding of a particular office;
  (c) the body has been recognised for the purpose of any enactment other than this Act and the recognition has not been withdrawn ...
(6) 'Enactment' includes an Act of the Scottish Parliament, Northern Ireland legislation and subordinate legislation (whether made under an Act, an Act of the Scottish Parliament or Northern Ireland legislation).
(7) 'Recognised' means recognised by–
  (a) a Minister of the Crown;
  (b) the Scottish Ministers;
  (c) a Northern Ireland Minister;
  (d) a Northern Ireland department or its head.

327 Exemption from the general prohibition

(1) The general prohibition does not apply to the carrying on of a regulated activity by a person ('P') if–
  (a) the conditions set out in subsections (2) to (7) are satisfied; **F1** ...
  [F2(aa) where the activity is the provision of a service listed in **[F3**Part 3 of Schedule 2 to the Financial Services and Markets Act 2000 (Regulated Activities) Order 2001]** relating to a financial instrument, the condition set out in subsection (7A) is also satisfied; and]**
  (b) there is not in force–
    (i) a direction under section 328, or
    (ii) an order under section 329,
  which prevents this subsection from applying to the carrying on of that activity by him.
(2) P must be–
  (a) a member of a profession; or
  (b) controlled or managed by one or more such members.
(3) P must not receive from a person other than his client any pecuniary reward or other advantage, for which he does not account to his client, arising out of his carrying on of any of the activities.
(4) The manner of the provision by P of any service in the course of carrying on the activities must be incidental to the provision by him of professional services.
(5) P must not carry on, or hold himself out as carrying on, a regulated activity other than–
  (a) one which rules made as a result of section 332(3) allow him to carry on; or
  (b) one in relation to which he is an exempt person.

(6) The activities must not be of a description, or relate to an investment of a description, specified in an order made by the Treasury for the purposes of this subsection.

(7) The activities must be the only regulated activities carried on by P (other than regulated activities in relation to which he is an exempt person).

[F4 (7A) The condition mentioned in subsection (1)(aa) is that—

    (a) the service is provided in an incidental manner in the course of a professional activity **F5** ...; and

    (b) the professional activity concerned is the provision of professional services.

(7B)   In subsection (7A) a service is provided in an incidental manner in the course of a professional activity **F6** ... if the applicable conditions are satisfied.

(7C)   The applicable conditions for the purposes of subsection (7B) are those set out in **[F7**paragraph 6(a) to (c) of Schedule 3 to the Financial Services and Markets Act 2000 (Regulated Activities) Order 2001**].]**.

(8) 'Professional services' means services-

    (a) which do not constitute carrying on a regulated activity, and

    (b) the provision of which is supervised and regulated by a designated professional body.

[F8 (9) The exemption in this section does not apply to the carrying on of a regulated claims management activity in Great Britain.**]**

328 Directions in relation to the general prohibition

(1) The **[F1**FCA**]** may direct that section 327(1) is not to apply to the extent specified in the direction.

(2) A direction under subsection (1)-

    (a) must be in writing;

    (b) may be given in relation to different classes of person or different descriptions of regulated activity.

(3) A direction under subsection (1) must be published in the way appearing to the **[F1**FCA**]** to be best calculated to bring it to the attention of the public.

(4) The **[F1**FCA**]** may charge a reasonable fee for providing a person with a copy of the direction.

(5) The **[F1**FCA**]** must, without delay, give the Treasury a copy of any direction which it gives under this section.

[F2 (6) The **[F1**FCA**]** may exercise the power conferred by subsection (1) only if it is satisfied **F3** ... —

    (a) that it is desirable to do so in order to protect the interests of clients ...

(7) In considering whether it is **[F6**satisfied of the matter specified in subsection (6) (a)]**, the **[F1**FCA**]** must have regard amongst other things to the effectiveness of any arrangements made by any designated professional body-

    (a) for securing compliance with rules made under section 332(1);

    (b) for dealing with complaints against its members in relation to the carrying on by them of exempt regulated activities;

    (c) in order to offer redress to clients who suffer, or claim to have suffered, loss as a result of misconduct by its members in their carrying on of exempt regulated activities;

    (d) for co-operating with the [FCA][1] under section 325(4).

(8) In this Part 'clients' means-

    (a) persons who use, have used or are or may be contemplating using, any of the services provided by a member of a profession in the course of carrying on exempt regulated activities;

    (b) persons who have rights or interests which are derived from, or otherwise attributable to, the use of any such services by other persons; or

    (c) persons who have rights or interests which may be adversely affected by the use of any such services by persons acting on their behalf or in a fiduciary capacity in relation to them.

(9) If a member of a profession is carrying on an exempt regulated activity in his capacity as a trustee, the persons who are, have been or may be beneficiaries of the trust are to be treated as persons who use, have used or are or may be contemplating using services provided by that person in his carrying on of that activity.

329 Orders in relation to the general prohibition

(1) Subsection (2) applies if it appears to the **[F1** FCA**]** that a person to whom, as a result of section 327(1), the general prohibition does not apply is not a fit and proper person to carry on regulated activities in accordance with that section.
(2) The **[F1** FCA**]** may make an order disapplying section 327(1) in relation to that person to the extent specified in the order.
(3) The **[F1** FCA**]** may, on the application of the person named in an order under subsection (1), vary or revoke it.
(4) 'Specified' means specified in the order.

332 Rules in relation to persons to whom the general prohibition does not apply

(1) The **[F1**FCA**]** may make rules applicable to persons to whom, as a result of section 327(1), the general prohibition does not apply.
(2) The power conferred by subsection (1) is to be exercised for the purpose of ensuring that clients are aware that such persons are not authorised persons.
(3) A designated professional body must make rules–
    (a) applicable to members of the profession in relation to which it is established who are not authorised persons; and
    (b) governing the carrying on by those members of regulated activities (other than regulated activities in relation to which they are exempt persons).
(4) Rules made in compliance with subsection (3) must be designed to secure that, in providing a particular professional service to a particular client, the member carries on only regulated activities which arise out of, or are complementary to, the provision by him of that service to that client.
(5) Rules made by a designated professional body under subsection (3) require the approval of the **[F1**FCA**]**.

*   *   *

Financial Services and Markets Act 2000 (Regulated Activities) Order 2001/544, arts 4, 21, 25, 29, 40, 53, 67, 73, 76, 77

Specified activities: general

4.—(1) The following provisions of this Part specify kinds of activity for the purposes of section 22 of the Act (and accordingly any activity of one of those kinds, which is carried on by way of business[1], and relates to an investment of a kind specified by any provision of Part III and applicable to that activity, is a regulated activity for the purposes of the Act).
(2) The kinds of activity specified by articles 51 and 52 are also specified for the purposes of section 22(1)(b) of the Act (and accordingly any activity of one of those kinds, when carried on by way of business, is a regulated activity when carried on in relation to property of any kind).

(3) Subject to paragraph (4), each provision specifying a kind of activity is subject to the exclusions applicable to that provision (and accordingly any reference in this Order to an activity of the kind specified by a particular provision is to be read subject to any such exclusions).

(4) Where an investment firm—

(a) provides core investment services to third parties on a professional basis, and

(b) in doing so would be treated as carrying on an activity of a kind specified by a provision of this Part but for an exclusion in any of articles 15, 68, 69 and 70, that exclusion is to be disregarded (and accordingly the investment firm is to be treated as carrying on an activity of the kind specified by the provision in question).

(5) In this article—

"core investment service" means any service listed in section A of the Annex to the investment services directive, the text of which is set out in Schedule 2; and "investment firm" means a person whose regular occupation or business is the provision of core investment services to third parties on a professional basis, other than—

(a) a person to whom the investment services directive does not apply by virtue of Article 2.2 of that directive (the text of which is set out in Schedule 3); or

(b) a person to whom (if he were incorporated in or formed under the law of an EEA State or, being an individual, had his head office in an EEA State) that directive would not apply by virtue of Article 2.2 of that directive.

---

[1] The Financial Services and Markets Act 2000 (Carrying on Regulated Activities by Way of Business) Order 2001 (S.I. 2001/), made under section 419 of the Act, makes provision as to the circumstances in which persons are, or are not, to be regarded as carrying on activities by way of business.

Dealing in investments as agent

21. Buying, selling, subscribing for or underwriting securities or contractually based investments (other than investments of the kind specified by article 87, or article 89 so far as relevant to that article) as agent is a specified kind of activity.

Arranging deals in investments

25.—(1) Making arrangements for another person (whether as principal or agent) to buy, sell, subscribe for or underwrite a particular investment which is—

(a) a security,

(b) a contractually based investment, or

(c) an investment of the kind specified by article 86, or article 89 so far as relevant to that article, is a specified kind of activity.

(2) Making arrangements with a view to a person who participates in the arrangements buying, selling, subscribing for or underwriting investments falling within paragraph (1)(a), (b) or (c) (whether as principal or agent) is also a specified kind of activity.

Arranging deals with or through authorised persons

29.—(1) There are excluded from article 25(1) and (2) arrangements made by a person ("A") who is not an authorised person for or with a view to a transaction which is or is to be entered into by a person ("the client") with or though an authorised person if—

(a) the transaction is or is to be entered into on advice to the client by an authorised person, or

(b) it is clear, in all the circumstances, that the client, in his capacity as an investor, is not seeking and has not sought advice from A as to the merits of the client's entering into the transaction (or, if the client has sought such advice, A has declined to give it but has recommended that the client seek such advice from an authorised person).

(2) But the exclusion in paragraph (1) does not apply if A receives from any person other than the client any pecuniary reward or other advantage, for which he does not account to the client, arising out of his making the arrangements.

Safeguarding and administering investments

40.—(1) The activity consisting of both—
   (a) the safeguarding of assets belonging to another, and
   (b) the administration of those assets,
   or arranging for one or more other persons to carry on that activity, is a specified kind of activity if the condition in sub-paragraph (a) or (b) of paragraph (2) is met.

(2) The condition is that—
   (a) the assets consist of or include any investment which is a security or a contractually based investment; or
   (b) the arrangements for their safeguarding and administration are such that the assets may consist of or include such investments, and either the assets have at any time since 1st June 1997 done so, or the arrangements have at any time (whether before or after that date) been held out as ones under which such investments would be safeguarded and administered.

(3) For the purposes of this article—
   (a) it is immaterial that title to the assets safeguarded and administered is held in uncertificated form;
   (b) it is immaterial that the assets safeguarded and administered may be transferred to another person, subject to a commitment by the person safeguarding and administering them, or arranging for their safeguarding and administration, that they will be replaced by equivalent assets at some future date or when so requested by the person to whom they belong.

Advising on investments

53. Advising a person is a specified kind of activity if the advice is—
   (a) given to the person in his capacity as an investor or potential investor, or in his capacity as agent for an investor or a potential investor; and
   (b) advice on the merits of his doing any of the following (whether as principal or agent)—
      (i) buying, selling, subscribing for or underwriting a particular investment which is a security or a contractually based investment, or
      (ii) exercising any right conferred by such an investment to buy, sell, subscribe for or underwrite such an investment.

Activities carried on in the course of a profession or non-investment business

67.—(1) There is excluded from articles 21, 25(1) and (2), 40 and 53 any activity which—
   (a) is carried on in the course of carrying on any profession or business which does not otherwise consist of regulated activities; and
   (b) may reasonably be regarded as a necessary part of other services provided in the course of that profession or business.

(2) But the exclusion in paragraph (1) does not apply if the activity in question is remunerated separately from the other services.

Investments: general

73. The following kinds of investment are specified for the purposes of section 22 of the Act.

Shares etc.

76.—(1) Shares or stock in the share capital of—
  (a) any body corporate (wherever incorporated), and
  (b) any unincorporated body constituted under the law of a country or territory outside the United Kingdom.
(2) Paragraph (1) includes—
  (a) any shares of a class defined as deferred shares for the purposes of section 119 of the Building Societies Act 1986[1]; and
  (b) any transferable shares in a body incorporated under the law of, or any part of, the United Kingdom relating to industrial and provident societies or credit unions, or in a body constituted under the law of another EEA State for purposes equivalent to those of such a body.
(3) But subject to paragraph (2) there are excluded from paragraph (1) shares or stock in the share capital of—
  (a) an open-ended investment company;
  (b) a building society incorporated under the law of, or any part of, the United Kingdom;
  (c) a body incorporated under the law of, or any part of, the United Kingdom relating to industrial and provident societies or credit unions;
  (d) any body constituted under the law of an EEA State for purposes equivalent to those of a body falling within sub-paragraph (b) or (c).

---

[1] 1986 c. 53.

Instruments creating or acknowledging indebtedness

77.—(1) Subject to paragraph (2), such of the following as do not fall within article 78—
  (a) debentures;
  (b) debenture stock;
  (c) loan stock;
  (d) bonds;
  (e) certificates of deposit;
  (f) any other instrument creating or acknowledging indebtedness.
(2) If and to the extent that they would otherwise fall within paragraph (1), there are excluded from that paragraph—
  (a) an instrument acknowledging or creating indebtedness for, or for money borrowed to defray, the consideration payable under a contract for the supply of goods or services;
  (b) a cheque or other bill of exchange, a banker's draft or a letter of credit (but not a bill of exchange accepted by a banker);
  (c) a banknote, a statement showing a balance on a current, deposit or savings account, a lease or other disposition of property, or a heritable security; and
  (d) a contract of insurance.
(3) An instrument excluded from paragraph (1) of article 78 by paragraph (2)(b) of that article is not thereby to be taken to fall within paragraph (1) of this article.

*   *   *

Source 4

Reproduced by permission of RELX (UK) Limited, trading as LexisNexis.

Halsbury's Laws of England **> Financial services regulation (Volume 50 (2022), paras 1–589; Volume 50A (2022), paras 590–1072) > 3. Regulated activities > (2) Regulated activities > (iii) Specified activities and exclusions > f. Dealing in investments > (C) Arranging deals, etc**

146. Arranging deals in investments

Making arrangements for another person (whether as principal or agent) to buy ..., sell ..., subscribe for or underwrite a particular investment which is a security ..., a relevant investment[4] or a specified investment[5], or a structured deposit ..., is a specified kind of activity[7].

This specified kind of activity is subject to the following exclusions: arrangements not causing a deal[8], arranging transactions to which the arranger is a party[9], arranging deals with or through authorised persons[10], arranging transactions in connection with lending on the security of insurance policies ..., arranging the acceptance of debentures in connection with loans ..., provision of information about contracts of insurance ..., arrangements for the issue of shares[14], international securities self-regulating organisations ..., and providing specified types of pensions guidance....

Making arrangements with a view to a person who participates in the arrangements buying, selling, subscribing for or underwriting such investments (whether as principal or agent) is also a specified kind of activity[17].

This specified kind of activity is subject to the following exclusions: enabling parties to communicate[18], arranging transactions to which the arranger is a party, arranging deals with or through authorised persons, arranging transactions in connection with lending on the security of insurance policies, arranging the acceptance of debentures in connection with loans, provision of finance[19], introducing[20], provision of information about contracts of insurance, arrangements for the issue of shares, international securities self-regulating organisations, securitisation repositories ..., trade repositories ..., and providing specified types of pensions guidance.

Neither activity above applies to the operation of a multilateral trading facility[23] or an organised trading facility[24].

A person is not to be regarded as carrying on by way of business[25] the activity of arranging deals in investments[26], unless he carries on the business of engaging in one or more such activities[27].

There are also other separate exclusions from the above specified activities[28] which relate to trustees[29], a profession or non-investment business[30], sale of goods and supply of services ..., groups and joint enterprises ..., sale of a body corporate ..., employee share schemes ..., overseas persons ..., activities carried on by a provider of relevant goods or services ..., provision of information on an incidental basis ..., a transitional exception for information society services ..., managers of UK UCITS and AIFs ..., large risks contracts where the risk is situated outside the United Kingdom ..., local authorities ..., insolvency practitioners ..., Business Angel-led Enterprise Capital

Funds ... and persons seeking to use the exemption in the Markets in Financial Instruments Directive....

---

4 As to the meaning of 'relevant investment' see PARA 143.

5 Ie an investment of the kind specified by the Financial Services and Markets Act 2000 (Regulated Activities) Order 2001, SI 2001/544, art 86 (Lloyd's syndicate capacity and syndicate membership) or art 89 (see PARA 271) so far as relevant to that article: see art 25(1)(c).

7 Financial Services and Markets Act 2000 (Regulated Activities) Order 2001, SI 2001/544, art 25(1) (amended by SI 2003/1476).

8 See the Financial Services and Markets Act 2000 (Regulated Activities) Order 2001, SI 2001/544, art 26; and PARA 153.

9 See the Financial Services and Markets Act 2000 (Regulated Activities) Order 2001, SI 2001/544, art 28; and PARA 155.

10 See the Financial Services and Markets Act 2000 (Regulated Activities) Order 2001, SI 2001/544, art 29; and PARA 157.

14 See the Financial Services and Markets Act 2000 (Regulated Activities) Order 2001, SI 2001/544, art 34; and PARA 165.

17 Financial Services and Markets Act 2000 (Regulated Activities) Order 2001, SI 2001/544, art 25(2). Article 25(2) was analysed in *FCA v Avacade [2020] EWHC 1673 (Ch)* from [193], where Adam Johnson QC (sitting as a Deputy High Court Judge) concluded that unregulated pension 'introducers' were carrying on regulated activities and that none of the exceptions applied (result affirmed on appeal: *[2021] EWCA Civ 1206, [2021] Bus LR 1810*).

18 See the Financial Services and Markets Act 2000 (Regulated Activities) Order 2001, SI 2001/544, art 27; and PARA 154.

19 See the Financial Services and Markets Act 2000 (Regulated Activities) Order 2001, SI 2001/544, art 28; and PARA 155.

20 See the Financial Services and Markets Act 2000 (Regulated Activities) Order 2001, SI 2001/544, art 33; and PARA 162.

23 Ie the activity in the Financial Services and Markets Act 2000 (Regulated Activities) Order 2001, SI 2001/544, art 25D:

24 Financial Services and Markets Act 2000 (Regulated Activities) Order 2001, SI 2001/544, art 25(3) (added by SI 2006/3384, amended by SI 2017/488). Operating an organised trading facility refers to the activity in Financial Services and Markets Act 2000 (Regulated Activities) Order 2001, SI 2001/544, art 25DA: see PARA 151.

25 See the Financial Services and Markets Act 2000 s 22 (see PARA 108) and s 419.

26 Ie either of the activities specified in the Financial Services and Markets Act 2000 (Regulated Activities) Order 2001, SI 2001/544, art 25(1) or (2).

27 Financial Services and Markets Act 2000 (Carrying on Regulated Activities by Way of Business) Order 2001, SI 2001/1177, art 3(1), (2) (amended by SI 2003/1476).

In relation to these activities, this applies except in so far as that activity relates to an investment of the kind specified by art 86 (Lloyd's syndicate capacity and syndicate membership), or art 89 (rights and interests) (see PARA 271): art 3(2).

The Financial Services and Markets Act 2000 (Carrying on Regulated Activities by Way of Business) Order 2001, SI 2001/1177, art 3(1) is without prejudice to art 4 in regard to occupational pension schemes (see PARA 171): art 3(3) (amended by SI 2003/1476). The Financial Services and Markets Act 2000 (Carrying on Regulated Activities by Way of Business) Order 2001, SI 2001/1177, is made under the Financial Services and Markets Act 2000 s 419.

28 Ie either of the activities specified in the Financial Services and Markets Act 2000 (Regulated Activities) Order 2001, SI 2001/544, art 25(1) or (2).

29 See the Financial Services and Markets Act 2000 (Regulated Activities) Order 2001, SI 2001/544, arts 36, 66.

30 See the Financial Services and Markets Act 2000 (Regulated Activities) Order 2001, SI 2001/544, arts 36, 67.

*   *   *

Source 5

Reproduced by permission of RELX (UK) Limited, trading as LexisNexis.

Halsbury's Laws of England > Financial services regulation (Volume 50 (2022), paras 1–589; Volume 50A (2022), paras 590–1072) > 3. Regulated activities > (2) Regulated activities > (iii) Specified activities and exclusions > zb. Exclusions applying to several activities

255 Exclusion for activities carried on in the course of a profession or non-investment business

There is excluded from the specified activity[1] of
  (1) dealing in investments as agent[2];
  (2) arranging deals in investments[3];
  (3) arranging regulated mortgage contracts[4];
  (4) arranging regulated home reversion plans[5];
  (5) arranging regulated home purchase plans[6];
  (6) arranging regulated sale and rent back agreements[7];
  (7) assisting in the administration and performance of a contract of insurance[8];
  (8) safeguarding and administering investments[9];
  (9) advising on investments[10];
 (10) advising on regulated mortgage contract[11];
 (11) advising on regulated home reversion plans[12];
 (12) advising on regulated home purchase plans[13];
 (13) advising on regulated sale and rent back agreements[14];
 (14) advising on regulated credit agreements for the acquisition of land[15],
      any activity which:
    (a) is carried on in the course of carrying on any profession or business which does not otherwise consist of the carrying on of regulated activities in the United Kingdom[16]; and
    (b) may reasonably be regarded as a necessary part of other services provided in the course of that profession or business[17].

However, this exclusion does not apply if the activity in question is remunerated separately from the other services[18].

---

[1] A 'specified activity' is an activity of a kind specified by the Financial Services and Markets Act 2000 (Regulated Activities) Order 2001, SI 2001/544, which is carried on by way of business, and relates to an investment of a kind specified by that Order and applicable to that activity, and is therefore a regulated activity for the purposes of the Financial Services and Markets Act 2000 s 22(1): see PARAS 108, 114.

[2] Ie excluded from the Financial Services and Markets Act 2000 (Regulated Activities) Order 2001, SI 2001/544, art 21 (see PARA 143): see arts 24, 67(1) (art 24 amended by SI 2002/1776; SI 2003/1476; SI 2013/1773; SI 2019/632; and SI 2019/1361; Financial Services and Markets Act 2000 (Regulated Activities) Order 2001, SI 2001/544, art 67(1) amended by SI 2003/1475, SI 2006/2383; SI 2009/1342; SI 2015/910).

[3] Ie excluded from the Financial Services and Markets Act 2000 (Regulated Activities) Order 2001, SI 2001/544, art 25(1), (2) (see PARA 146): see arts 36, 67(1) (art 36 amended by SI 2002/1776; SI 2003/1475; SI 2003/1476; SI 2006/2383; SI 2006/3384; SI 2009/1342; SI 2013/1773; SI 2014/366; SI 2015/910; SI 2019/632; SI 2019/1361).

[4] Ie excluded from the Financial Services and Markets Act 2000 (Regulated Activities) Order 2001, SI 2001/544, art 25A (see PARA 147): see arts 36, 67(1).

[5] Ie excluded from the Financial Services and Markets Act 2000 (Regulated Activities) Order 2001, SI 2001/544, art 25B (see PARA 148): see arts 36, 67(1).
[6] Ie excluded from the Financial Services and Markets Act 2000 (Regulated Activities) Order 2001, SI 2001/544, art 25C (see PARA 149): see arts 36, 67(1).
[7] Ie excluded from the Financial Services and Markets Act 2000 (Regulated Activities) Order 2001, SI 2001/544, art 25E (see PARA 152): see arts 36, 67(1).
[8] Ie excluded from the Financial Services and Markets Act 2000 (Regulated Activities) Order 2001, SI 2001/544, art 39A (see PARA 133): see arts 39C, 67(1) (art 39C added by SI 2003/1476; amended by SI 2013/1773; SI 2014/366; SI 2019/632; and SI 2019/1361).
[9] Ie excluded from the Financial Services and Markets Act 2000 (Regulated Activities) Order 2001, SI 2001/544, art 40 (see PARA 173): see arts 44, 67(1) (art 44 amended by SI 2002/1776; SI 2003/1476; SI 2013/1773; SI 2014/366; SI 2019/632; and SI 2019/1361).
[10] Ie excluded from the Financial Services and Markets Act 2000 (Regulated Activities) Order 2001, SI 2001/544, art 53 (see PARA 184): see arts 55, 67(1) (art 55 amended by SI 2002/1776; SI 2003/1475; SI 2006/2383; SI 2009/1342; SI 2013/1476; SI 2013/1773; SI 2014/366; SI 2015/910; SI 2019/632; SI 2019/1361).
[11] Ie excluded from the Financial Services and Markets Act 2000 (Regulated Activities) Order 2001, SI 2001/544, art 53A (see PARA 185): see arts 55, 67(1).
[12] Ie excluded from the Financial Services and Markets Act 2000 (Regulated Activities) Order 2001, SI 2001/544, art 53B (see PARA 186): see arts 55, 67(1).
[13] Ie excluded from the Financial Services and Markets Act 2000 (Regulated Activities) Order 2001, SI 2001/544, art 53C (see PARA 187): see arts 55, 67(1).
[14] Ie excluded from the Financial Services and Markets Act 2000 (Regulated Activities) Order 2001, SI 2001/544, art 53D (see PARA 188): see arts 55, 67(1).
[15] Ie excluded from the Financial Services and Markets Act 2000 (Regulated Activities) Order 2001, SI 2001/544, art 53DA (see PARA 189): see arts 55, 67(1).
[16] Financial Services and Markets Act 2000 (Regulated Activities) Order 2001, SI 2001/544, art 67(1)(a) (amended by SI 2001/3544). As to the meaning of 'United Kingdom' see PARA 2. The Financial Services and Markets Act 2000 (Regulated Activities) Order 2001, SI 2001/544, art 67 is subject to art 4(4), (4A), (4B) (see PARA 115 et seq): art 67(3) (added by SI 2006/3384; and amended by SI 2015/910).
[17] Financial Services and Markets Act 2000 (Regulated Activities) Order 2001, SI 2001/544, art 67(1)(b).
[18] Financial Services and Markets Act 2000 (Regulated Activities) Order 2001, SI 2001/544, art 67(2).

* * *

Source 6

Contains public sector information licensed under the Open Government Licence v3.0.

The Companies (Model Articles) Regulations 2008

Schedule 1 Model Articles for Private Companies Limited by Shares

Part 3

Unclaimed distributions

33 (1) All dividends or other sums which are—
    (a) payable in respect of shares, and
    (b) unclaimed after having been declared or become payable,
    may be invested or otherwise made use of by the directors for the benefit of the company until claimed.

(2) The payment of any such dividend or other sum into a separate account does not make the company a trustee in respect of it.

(3) If—

(a) twelve years have passed from the date on which a dividend or other sum became due for payment, and

(b) the distribution recipient has not claimed it,

the distribution recipient is no longer entitled to that dividend or other sum and it ceases to remain owing by the company.

Non-cash distributions

34 (1) Subject to the terms of issue of the share in question, the company may, by ordinary resolution on the recommendation of the directors, decide to pay all or part of a dividend or other distribution payable in respect of a share by transferring non-cash assets of equivalent value (including, without limitation, shares or other securities in any company).

(2) For the purposes of paying a non-cash distribution, the directors may make whatever arrangements they think fit, including, where any difficulty arises regarding the distribution—

(a) fixing the value of any assets;

(b) paying cash to any distribution recipient on the basis of that value in order to adjust the rights of recipients; and

(c) vesting any assets in trustees.

Waiver of distributions

35 Distribution recipients may waive their entitlement to a dividend or other distribution payable in respect of a share by giving the company notice in writing to that effect, but if—

(a) the share has more than one holder, or

(b) more than one person is entitled to the share, whether by reason of the death or bankruptcy of one or more joint holders, or otherwise,

the notice is not effective unless it is expressed to be given, and signed, by all the holders or persons otherwise entitled to the share.

Schedule 3 Model Articles for Public Companies

Part 4

Unclaimed distributions

75 (1) All dividends or other sums which are—

(a) payable in respect of shares, and

(b) unclaimed after having been declared or become payable,

may be invested or otherwise made use of by the directors for the benefit of the company until claimed.

(2) The payment of any such dividend or other sum into a separate account does not make the company a trustee in respect of it.

(3) If—

(a) twelve years have passed from the date on which a dividend or other sum became due for payment, and

(b) the distribution recipient has not claimed it,

the distribution recipient is no longer entitled to that dividend or other sum and it ceases to remain owing by the company.

Non-cash distributions

76 (1) Subject to the terms of issue of the share in question, the company may, by ordinary resolution on the recommendation of the directors, decide to pay all or part of a dividend or other distribution payable in respect of a share by transferring non-cash assets of equivalent value (including, without limitation, shares or other securities in any company).

(2) If the shares in respect of which such a non-cash distribution is paid are uncertificated, any shares in the company which are issued as a non-cash distribution in respect of them must be uncertificated.

(3) For the purposes of paying a non-cash distribution, the directors may make whatever arrangements they think fit, including, where any difficulty arises regarding the distribution—

(a) fixing the value of any assets;

(b) paying cash to any distribution recipient on the basis of that value in order to adjust the rights of recipients; and

(c) vesting any assets in trustees.

Waiver of distributions

77 Distribution recipients may waive their entitlement to a dividend or other distribution payable in respect of a share by giving the company notice in writing to that effect, but if—

(a) the share has more than one holder, or

(b) more than one person is entitled to the share, whether by reason of the death or bankruptcy of one or more joint holders, or otherwise,

the notice is not effective unless it is expressed to be given, and signed, by all the holders or persons otherwise entitled to the share.

*   *   *

■ YOUR TURN

Have a go at answering question 2.
- Make sure that you address each point in the assessment criteria (see page 34).
- Use the five steps on page 37 as a method for approaching the assessment.
- Structure your answer around the headings suggested on page 59, but remember to remove the headings at the end of the assessment.
- Do not forget to time yourself. Timings are important: you will need to prepare and write your answer in 60 minutes.

SQE 1 Functioning legal knowledge link

This question focuses on business practice in the context of advising and arranging a deal in investments. If you need to review your knowledge of this area, it is covered in chapter 5 of **Revise SQE: Business Law and Practice** and chapter 4 of **Revise SQE: Ethics and Professional Conduct**.

EVALUATING YOUR ANSWER

Once you have attempted completing the report, mark it yourself against the SQE2 legal research assessment criteria. Do you think your attempt met the threshold standard?

Now compare your attempt with the following key legal points and two sample answers. A circled number indicates that commentary is provided for this part of the answer. The commentary will explain whether or not the sample is likely to meet the SQE2 standard threshold.

> ### ➥Key legal points: question 2
>
> In this assessment, part or all of the following sources are relevant to the question:
> 2.   Financial Services and Markets Act 2000, c 8 ss 19, 22, 23, 26, 325–9, 332
> 3.   Financial Services and Markets Act 2000 (Regulated Activities) Order 2001/544 arts 4, 21, 25, 29, 40, 53, 67, 73, 76, 77
> 4.   *Halsbury's Laws of England*, Financial Services Regulation, vol. 50 (2022), para 146
> 5.   *Halsbury's Laws of England*, Financial Services Regulation, vol. 50 (2022), para 255.
>
> The following sources are not relevant to the question:
> 1.   Companies Act 2006, c 46 ss 733, 734
> 6.   The Companies (Model Articles) Regulations 2008, arts 33–5, 75–7.
>
> Your FLK from SQE1 should lead you to make the following legal points from your research:
> - The SRA requires all providers of legal services to understand what financial advice they may or may not offer to their clients.
> - Law firms and individuals must be able to advise their clients on how certain transactions may be regulated by the Financial Services and Markets Act 2000.
> - There is a general prohibition under s 19(1) of the Financial Services and Markets Act 2000.
> - A regulated activity is defined by s 22(1) of the Financial Services and Markets Act 2000.
> - Article 25 of the Financial Services and Markets Act 2000 (Regulated Activities) Order 2001/544 states that arranging deals in investments includes making arrangements for another person (whether as principal or agent) to buy, sell, subscribe for or underwrite a particular investment which is a security (share).
> - Article 67 of the Financial Services and Markets Act 2000 (Regulated Activities) Order 2001/544 outlines activity carried on during profession or business does not consist of the carrying on of regulated activities. This means it can be reasonably regarded as a necessary part of other services provided during that profession or business. Therefore, it will be excluded from the specified kind under s 22 of the Financial Services and Markets Act 2000.

Now let's consider the first sample answer to question 2. You will note that the answer contains headings in square brackets and italics, which have been added so you can see how the answer is applied to the logical structure guidance on page 59. We would suggest that these headings are removed before the answer is submitted.

■ SAMPLE ANSWER 1 TO QUESTION 2

[Background]

IG Ltd (a private company) wants to purchase 100 buyback shares which are being sold by a shareholder. The company was advised of the procedural requirements they need to satisfy under the Companies Act 2006. The company has instructed us to arrange the buyback of shares by generating the relevant documents. ❶

[What I have researched]

I have researched whether this constitutes arranging a deal in investments, which is a regulated activity. I understand the firm is neither an authorised nor exempt person under s 19(1) of the Financial Services and Markets Act 2000. I have concluded that the advice given does not constitute 'arranging a deal in investments'. ❷

[Advice and legal reasoning]

Halsbury's Laws of England, Financial Services Regulation, vol. 50 (2022), para 255 defines a regulated activity. Regulated activity under s 22(1) of the Financial Services and Markets Act 2000 is an activity of a specified kind which is carried on in the way of business and relates to an investment of a specified kind.

Halsbury's Laws of England, Financial Services Regulation, vol. 50 (2022), para 146 outlines that arranging deals in investments is excluded from the specified activity.

Article 25 of the Financial Services and Markets Act 2000 (Regulated Activities) Order 2001/544 states that arranging deals in investments includes making arrangements for another person (whether as principal or agent) to buy, sell, subscribe for or underwrite a particular investment which is a security (share). This is a specified kind of activity. It further states that making arrangements with a view to a person who participates in the arrangements buying, selling, subscribing for or underwriting investments is also a specified kind of activity.

Article 67 of the Financial Services and Markets Act 2000 (Regulated Activities) Order 2001/544 specifies that any activity which is carried on during profession or business, which does not otherwise consist of the carrying on of regulated activities in the United Kingdom, and may reasonably be regarded as a necessary part of other services provided in the course of that profession or business, will be excluded from the specified kind under s 22 of the Financial Services and Markets Act 2000. However, this exclusion does not apply if the activity in question is remunerated separately from the other services. This exclusion is subject to art 4(4) of the Financial Services and Markets Act 2000 (Regulated Activities) Order 2001/544. ❸

[Conclusion/Next steps]

Both actions you have completed are excluded as being an activity of a specified kind under art 67 of the Financial Services and Markets Act 2000 (Regulated Activities) Order 2001/544, because they can be reasonably regarded as a necessary part of other services provided in the course of the business. ❹

In addition, when a company is buying back its own shares from a selling shareholder, the company is not purchasing those shares in the capacity of an investor. This means that investment advice has not been provided either. ❺

COMMENTARY

❶ The initial paragraph outlines what was discussed in the meeting. This is useful because it sets out the factual background to which the law is being applied. It is important to provide this summary as it explains the basis of the legal advice. This adheres to point 1 in the suggested structure provided in our Assessment technique box on page 59.

❷ This paragraph explains what has been researched in a clear, precise and concise way. The partner at the firm is looking for a summary of the advice which is quick and easy to read and understand. In this case the partner will need to report back to the managing director quickly to resolve the issue. This adheres to point 2 in the suggested structure provided in our Assessment technique box on page 59.

❸ These four paragraphs outline the advice and legal reasoning. This adheres to point 3 in the suggested structure provided in our Assessment technique box on page 59. The candidate has pinpointed the key words and phrases and looked them up in the secondary sources, which has led them to the correct legislation. The candidate has demonstrated an ability to assess which sources are relevant and apply the law. The reader of this email is a partner, and the advice is being passed on to the managing director who has some knowledge of the Financial Services and Markets Act 2000. It is therefore appropriate to quote the relevant legislation and use legal terminology such as specified activity; the candidate is using appropriate language here.

❹ This paragraph outlines the conclusion and adheres to point 4 in the suggested structure provided in our Assessment technique box on page 59. In this question, the next steps are not necessary, but they may be applicable in other questions. The answer is concisely set out with a link to the relevant primary legal source.

❺ This point has not been specifically asked in the email, but here the candidate demonstrates their ability to identify other professional conduct concerns the managing director may have; this satisfies assessment criterion 5. The managing director is clearly worried about breaches of the Financial Services and Markets Act 2000. By including this information, the candidate provides a recipient-focused approach which anticipates and deals with potential issues.

Does this answer meet the threshold?

The sample answer correctly identifies that a law firm is an excluded person under art 67 of the Financial Services and Markets Act 2000 (Regulated Activities) Order 2001 because it can be reasonably regarded as carrying out the activity as a necessary part of other services provided in the course of the business. The candidate also identifies that the company will not be deemed as acting in the capacity of an investor because it is buying back shares, and therefore the partner has not provided advice on investments. This shows an accurate application of the law, and the candidate has correctly identified that Sources 1 and 6 are not relevant. The answer is thus likely to meet the threshold standard for SQE2 legal research.

Now consider the second sample answer to question 2.

■ SAMPLE ANSWER 2 TO QUESTION 2

The advice you have given constitutes 'arranging a deal in investments'. ❶

The advice you have given to the client included informing them why they should buy back the shares, what they need to comply with to facilitate a buyback of shares under the Companies Act 2006 and how to generate the relevant documents to facilitate that buyback. During the meeting you also recommended some other share options on the Market, including shares in a specific public limited company (PLC). ❷

These actions are excluded as being an activity of a specified kind under art 67 of the Financial Services and Markets Act 2000 (Regulated Activities) Order 2001 because they can be reasonably regarded as a necessary part of other services provided in the course of the business. ❸

Financial Services and Markets Act 2000, c 8
This is a primary resource which contains relevant legislation.

Financial Services and Markets Act 2000 (Regulated Activities) Order 2001/544
This is a primary resource which contains relevant legislation.

Companies Act 2006, c 46
This is a primary resource which contains relevant legislation.

Halsbury's Laws of England, Financial Services Regulation, vol. 50 (2022), para 146
This is a secondary resource which contains relevant information.

Halsbury's Laws of England, Financial Services Regulation, vol. 50 (2022), para 255)
This is a secondary resource which contains relevant information.

The Companies (Model Articles) Regulations 2008
This is a primary resource which contains relevant information. ❹

COMMENTARY

❶ This is incorrect. The advice discussed in the question is likely to satisfy art 67 of the Financial Services and Markets Act 2000 (Regulated Activities) Order 2001. This means that the activity will be excluded because it was carried out in the course of carrying on a profession, and may be reasonably regarded as a necessary part of other professional services. Simply put, if the solicitor is ensuring compliance with the Companies Act 2006 requirements relating to the company buyback of the shares, then it is likely that art 67 will apply.

❷ This paragraph contains inaccurate and misleading information about what was discussed in the meeting. This is problematic because it means the outcome of the research advice will be incorrect. This has wider implications as it is a breach of Rule 1.4 SRA Code of Conduct for Firms, which states a solicitor must not mislead a client, the court or others. This paragraph also mentions giving specific advice about shares in a specific company. This is incorrect information, but if it were true, this would be a breach of the Financial Services and Markets Act 2000 and would significantly alter the advice.

❸ Had the discussion about Pear PLC been excluded, the information in this paragraph would have been correct. However, as discussed above, if the solicitor did give advice about investing in shares in a specific company, this would be a breach and is unlikely to satisfy the exclusion in art 67 of the Financial Services and Markets Act 2000 (Regulated Activities) Order 2001. This paragraph also contradicts other information given in this answer.

❹ This is a poor attempt to provide legal reasoning. The candidate has included all the sources, which does not demonstrate an ability to identify only relevant sources. The candidate also does not discuss any specific parts of those sources or explain the principles and why they are important. Instead, all that has been included is a definition of the type of source, either primary or secondary.

Does this answer meet the threshold?

It is unlikely that this answer would meet the threshold standard for SQE2 legal research. The answer is very short, and there is insufficient exploration of the law or application to the facts. When checked against the SQE2 legal research assessment criteria, we can see that this answer does not identify and use relevant sources, and as noted in the commentary, irrelevant sources have been included. The general approach of this sample answer is misguided, and includes incorrect facts which could show negligence in practice. Because of this, the advice is not client-focused and the appropriate ethical and professional conduct issues cannot be raised, which negatively impacts the advice provided.

■ KEY POINT CHECKLIST

This chapter has covered the following key knowledge points:
• The SQE2 assessment criteria for legal research, and applying it in the context of professional conduct issues regarding the provision of financial services.
• A suggested structure for approaching an SQE2 legal research question.
• Sample answers that show what is likely or unlikely to meet the Day One Solicitor competency.

■ SUMMARY AND REFLECTION

The key to success in the SQE2 legal research assessment is proactive time management. You will need to strategise when reviewing the sources to make sure you identify the ones most relevant to the research question. The stepped approach shown in this chapter should lead you to evaluate the sources correctly and identify the relevant ones for addressing the client's problem.

Remember that you are being assessed on your ability to produce a research note that is precise and uses acceptable language. Make sure that you clearly report your answer to the research issue, and demonstrate how you have found that answer by quoting the relevant sources.

Before moving on to the next chapter, take some time to reflect and consider what you might still need to work on, and whether you feel completely confident in your legal research skills.

3

Legal writing

■ INTRODUCTION TO LEGAL WRITING

This chapter explores the legal skill of writing. To pass the SRA's writing skills centralised assessment for SQE2, you must demonstrate that you can produce written work that meets the SRA's standard of competency of a Day One Solicitor. Whilst you may have some experience of writing letters in practice, this does not mean that you are meeting the criteria set by the SRA. It is therefore crucial that your revision is focused on what the SRA's expectations are of a Day One Solicitor.

First, this chapter will explain in more detail what legal writing is and why it is an important legal skill for a solicitor. It will then explore how legal writing is assessed for SQE2, providing a detailed commentary on the assessment criteria against which your work will be marked. This is followed by a stepped approach to legal writing in the context of a property practice case study (question 1) and two sample answers for you to scrutinise. Thereafter, you will have the opportunity to practise your own legal writing skills for question 2, which is in the context of business practice, and produce your own answer. Again, two sample answers are provided which you can use to reflect on your own answer.

WHAT IS LEGAL WRITING, AND WHY IS IT AN IMPORTANT SKILL FOR A SOLICITOR?

Legal writing focuses on the skill of communicating legal information or advice to a client or another professional. It usually takes the form of a letter, but it can come in alternative forms, such as a report or memorandum to present the results of legal research.

Legal writing is a vital skill in practice and not to be underestimated. It is crucial that you are able to communicate advice effectively in written form and include relevant information, to avoid negative repercussions for your client or yourself. You should be able to convey information and advice in a way that avoids ambiguity and confusion, and is persuasive and authoritative.

You will need to develop clear, concise and precise language skills for both written and verbal communication. In legal practice you will be required to communicate with a variety of different people, and it is important that you are able to adopt the appropriate tone and vocabulary for your recipient.

HOW IS LEGAL WRITING ASSESSED IN SQE2?

The SQE2 written centralised assessments take place over three half-days. You will be assessed on your legal writing skills on each day:
• Day one – in the context of dispute resolution or criminal litigation.

- Day two – in the context of property practice or wills and intestacy, probate administration and practice.
- Day three – in the context of business organisations, rules and procedures.

In the assessment, you will complete a 30-minute computer-based assessment which requires you, as a competent, qualified Day One Solicitor, to write a letter or email to a recipient. You will need to demonstrate that you can apply the correct law to the client's issue and adopt the appropriate language and writing style for the reader.

You will be provided with a memorandum in the form of an email from a partner, explaining what advice is required. The email might be accompanied by other documents relating to the matter. The recipient of your letter or email could be anyone, although it is likely to be:
- a client
- a third party
- the other side to litigation or to a client transaction, or
- a partner within your firm's organisation.

Your writing style will need to be appropriate to the specific recipient and address the recipient's goals or concerns by outlining the relevant legal position.

The letter might be in the context of a negotiation. This may mean that you will need to include a 'Without prejudice' label (which is discussed in further detail on page 90).

At the end of the email/memorandum from the partner, there might be a 'Note to candidates'. Make sure you read this carefully, as it will give you guidance about what you do not need to discuss in your letter.

You will complete your letter on an electronic template which will be provided. The template includes the recipient's address. However, please remember that the template is solely for the purposes of assessment and does not fulfil all the legal requirements for business stationery. Compliance with this legal requirement is not part of the assessment, and you should not attempt to amend what is already included on the template.

■ ASSESSMENT CRITERIA AND COMMENTARY

As you prepare your answer in the SQE2 assessment for legal writing, remember that it will be judged against the following criteria:

SQE2 legal writing assessment criteria

Skills assessment criteria

1. Include relevant facts.
2. Use a logical structure.
3. Make sure advice/content is client- and recipient-focused.
4. Use clear, precise, concise and acceptable language which is appropriate to the recipient.

Application of law assessment criteria

5. Apply the law correctly to the client's situation.
6 Apply the law comprehensively to the client's situation, identifying any ethical and professional conduct issues and exercising judgment to resolve them honestly and with integrity.

Let's look more closely at each point in these criteria, and explore the SRA's standard of competency as detailed in their performance indicators for SQE2 legal writing.

SKILLS ASSESSMENT CRITERIA

1. Include relevant facts

You will already be aware of the importance of noting relevant and irrelevant facts from studying the legal skill of case and matter analysis in Chapter 1. The emphasis on identifying relevant facts is the same for legal writing.

You will demonstrate **competence** if you include relevant facts from your instructions.
* You should include a short summary of the factual background at the beginning of your legal writing assessment, especially where you are basing your legal advice on that information.
* If you are asked to give advice on the basis of a client's objective, you need to demonstrate in your response that you have considered that specific information when forming your advice.

You will **not** demonstrate **competence** if you have included a variety of facts that have no bearing on your legal advice and are thus irrelevant to the legal issue.

2. Use a logical structure

For a piece of legal writing to be logically structured, it needs to flow in a way that makes sense. You may find it helpful to use headings when structuring your work, especially when you first start to practise writing legal letters.

When it comes to formatting your letter, do not worry if this is something you are unsure about. The SRA has confirmed that you will not be penalised for poorly formatted letters, because there is a lack of formatting support on the SQE2 assessment test platform. Remember that you only have 30 minutes for this assessment, so you need to concentrate on writing rather than formatting.

You will demonstrate **competence** if you present your letter in a clear, well-organised structure. Legal letters are often lengthy and difficult for clients to understand. It is therefore very important that your letter is easy to follow and understandable from the reader's perspective.

You will **not** demonstrate **competence** if the presentation:
* is confused, and difficult to follow or understand
* repeats the same point
* focuses on irrelevant issues.

For recommendations on how to structure your legal letter, see pages 99–100.

3. Make sure advice/content is client- and recipient-focused

In practice you will be in situations where you must give clients unwelcome advice. It is never easy to give difficult advice, and you will need to develop the skill of communicating empathically and with sensitivity, both in person and in writing.

> ### Code of Conduct for Solicitors, RELs and RFLs link
>
> Whilst no one likes delivering bad news, as per the Code of Conduct for Solicitors, RELs and RFLs, you must not mislead or attempt to mislead your clients (rule 1.4). Therefore, you must be comfortable being the bearer of bad news and avoid giving false hope which could mislead a client.
>
> See page 15 for a summary of the Code of Conduct.

You will demonstrate **competence** if you:
- demonstrate an understanding of the client's problem from their perspective
- address any relevant commercial considerations
- address the client's personal circumstances, priorities, objectives and constraints
- explore options and provide advice on strategies and solutions. This will not be relevant in every scenario, but the SRA has said that you may need to give advice in the context of negotiation. Please see page 14 for information about negotiating.

When writing your legal letter, you will need to consider who the client is and what their key issues are. You can then consider any risks for the client, bearing in mind that businesses and individual clients might have very different interests and risks.

You will **not** demonstrate **competence** if you:
- demonstrate that you do not understand the client's perspective
- focus on irrelevant issues
- fail to provide appropriate advice
- fail to advise the client on solutions, strategies and relevant options
- do not consider who the client is, or recognise their key issues and any risks in this case
- lack empathy or sensitivity in your writing when imparting any difficult or unwelcome news.

A further consideration when providing client-focused advice is to use appropriate labels. This can also be helpful to show that you have applied the law comprehensively to the client's situation, identified any ethical and professional conduct issues and exercised judgement to resolve them honestly and with integrity. This may not always be relevant to the scenario given, but here are some examples where it may be appropriate to add a label:
- If you are sending a legal letter with confidential and sensitive content to a client, you might need to label the letter 'Private and confidential'. This emphasises that only the intended recipient should read the letter.
- In dispute resolution cases, there may be circumstances where you will need to mark a letter 'Without prejudice'. This means that parties can enter into negotiations by making offers or discuss settling claims without those offers and discussions becoming known to a judge. Those discussions cannot be used against a party, should a settlement attempt fail.
- In property cases, you may need to mark a letter 'Subject to contract'. This label means the parties are still negotiating and are yet to reach a final binding agreement.

4. Use clear, precise, concise and acceptable language which is appropriate to the recipient

For a reminder of what clear, precise, concise and acceptable language means, please see Chapter 1, page 5. See also the Assessment technique box on the same page for advice on spelling and grammar.

Take particular care when referring to names of clients and companies from the question:
- The misspelt name of a company could impact the result from a Companies House search.
- Misspelling a client's name would not inspire trust and confidence in practice.

You will demonstrate **competence** if you:
- use understandable language which has a clarity of expression
- base your choice of words on the identity of the reader
- avoid using unnecessary technical terms and legal jargon.

You will **not** demonstrate **competence** if:
- the reader would struggle to understand your use of language, which can occur if your answer lacks clarity or is poorly expressed
- the reader's understanding is adversely affected by the density, length or brevity of the answer.

Letter writing for the SQE2 assessment is very different from essay writing at undergraduate level. Make sure you do not muddle the different styles, as they have different purposes and effects: an essay is intended to be an analytical explorative piece of work, whereas a legal letter is intended to provide advice.

> **Assessment technique**
>
> When negotiating in a legal letter, try to be subtle when making allegations, especially to the person who can offer a settlement agreement. If you are neutral when setting out the facts and do not include emotive language, this will make you appear more professional.

APPLICATION OF LAW ASSESSMENT CRITERIA

5. Apply the law correctly to the client's situation

The SRA has produced a list of content which they may examine you on for dispute resolution, criminal litigation, property practice, wills and intestacy, probate administration and practice, and business organisations, rules and procedures. You will find this information on the SRA website. We recommend that you familiarise yourself with those topics.

You will demonstrate **competence** if you can identify the relevant fundamental legal principles and apply them correctly.

You will **not** demonstrate **competence** if you
- do not identify the relevant legal principles
- do not correctly apply those legal principles to the client's case in a way that addresses their needs and concerns.

6. Apply the law comprehensively to the client's situation

You need to identify any ethical and professional conduct issues and exercise judgement to resolve them honestly and with integrity.

You will see that all of the questions throughout this book are based on ethical and professional conduct issues. We have clearly identified the ethical and professional conduct issue; however, in the SQE2 assessment the ethical and professional conduct issue will not be made explicit. Make sure you revise the guidance provided in this book to help you spot such issues in the SQE2 assessment.

You will demonstrate **competence** under these circumstances:
- Your legal analysis is 'sufficiently detailed' in the context of the client's case. To achieve this, you need to demonstrate that you can evaluate relevant information to identify key issues and risks, and can reach reasonable conclusions which are supported by appropriate evidence.
- You refer to pertinent ethical issues and/or the SRA Principles and rules of professional conduct.

You will **not** demonstrate **competence** under these circumstances:
- Your analysis is not 'sufficiently detailed' – ie you demonstrate little or no understanding of the key issues and risks, and do not reach reasonable conclusions as you have failed to apply the law to the facts.
- You do not refer to pertinent ethical issues and/or the SRA Principles and rules of professional conduct.

■ A STEPPED APPROACH TO LEGAL WRITING

Legal writing for the SQE2 assessment can be broken down into three basic steps:
1.   Establish the relevant content that must be included.
2.   Structure your response in a logical way.
3.   Ensure that the style and language of the letter is appropriate for the reader.

Let's now work through question 1 and break down the steps to complete a legal letter. This stepped approach will help you to meet the SRA's assessment criteria, which is crucial to your success in this assessment. Question 1 focuses on possible money laundering within the context of a conveyancing case.

■ QUESTION 1

Email to candidate

From: Alexander Thomas (Partner)
Sent: 19 January 202#
To: Candidate
Subject: Mrs Daisy Brooks (purchase of 28 Lakeview Way, Nottingham, NG5 8PL. Current address: 42 Orchard Crescent, Weston, NG24 7DG)

I met Mrs Daisy Brooks yesterday afternoon in relation to a house purchase. Mrs Brooks is purchasing 28 Lakeview Way, Nottingham, NG5 8PL with her husband, Mr Jude Brooks (I have not spoken to him yet).

I took a photocopy of Mrs Brooks' ID before the meeting started and explained I would also need Mr Brooks' ID. Mrs Brooks and her husband own a number of businesses including restaurants, bars and a car wash company.

Mrs Brooks supplied all the required information in that meeting, and I have provided the attendance note for your consideration (Attachment 1). I explained our fees in that meeting and that we would send her a client care letter with a retainer for her and her husband to sign. She asked whether she could sign the retainer now because she is anxious to get things moving. I had a very lengthy meeting with her so I was happy to get the signature in person, but reminded her that I would still need her husband to sign the retainer.

When I was leaving work yesterday, I was made aware that money had been paid to the firm for Mrs Brooks' account. I didn't think anything of it at the time because I was in a rush to leave for the school run.

When I logged onto my emails today, I had received an email from the firm's accounts team confirming receipt of £21,000 from Martha Willis for the Brooks case. I thought this was odd because Mrs Brooks did not mention that a Martha Willis would be paying, and the sum credited far exceeds the 10% deposit and our costs.

I also saw that Mrs Brooks emailed me overnight asking that I return some of the money, and she sent me her bank details for the money to be returned to. She claims that Martha Willis is her cousin who owed her some money, and they agreed she would pay the solicitor as settlement of the debt. Mrs Brooks also sent me a faded picture of Mr Brooks' passport over email last night.

I am concerned that this could be an attempt at placement. We need to be careful that we do not commit a direct or indirect offence.

I have reported my suspicions to the firm's money laundering reporting officer. We have completed a Suspicious Client/Matter Report Form (Attachment 2), and he has made a Suspicious Activity Report to the National Crime Agency.

But, as Mrs Brooks is a new client, we still need to write to her. I have already sent a client care letter yesterday (18 January 202#), but I did not mention money laundering or acting for joint buyers.

1   **Please compose a letter for me to send which exclusively details advice on acting for joint buyers and the money laundering controls we need to adhere to.**
2   **Please remind her to sign and return the retainer in your letter.**

Remember that Mrs Brooks is not a lawyer, so it is important that you write clearly and concisely.

Thanks

Alexander Thomas, Partner

Attachment:

Attendance Note and Report Form

Note to candidates:

Please assume that the client case letter has included everything on the SRA client care letter checklist, including information about who is to carry out the work, costs, service standards, a summary of the advice given, information required and information about the complaints procedure.

Attachment 1

Attendance note

File: Brooks/BR28L
Client: Mrs Daisy Brooks
Date: 18 January 202#
Time attending: 10 units

New client: Daisy Brooks. Client ID was obtained during the meeting. Proof of address yet to be provided.
DOB: 07/09/1961
Current address: 42 Orchard Crescent, Weston, NG24 7DG
Occupation: Business owner. Businesses include Darla Dinning Restaurants, Hilltop View Café, Jazz Nights Bar, Hop Bar and Car Wax & Wash.
Mobile number: 07765876115
Email address: ddbrooks@gmail.com
Bank details:
Spouse: Mr Jude Brooks. ID outstanding.
Mrs Brooks has instructed the firm to act for her and her husband ('the clients') in the purchase of 'the Property', 28 Lakeview Way, Nottingham, NG5 8PL. This is a residential registered freehold property and will be the new family home. The

client understands that the Property is approximately 40 years old. We will confirm this once we have received official copies. The purchase price of the Property is £120,000.

The Property is currently owned by Mr and Mrs Parsons. They are represented by Slattery Solicitors (contact details already on file). The estate agents are Walker & Walker (contact details already on file).

No synchronised sale. They will not be selling their current home. Instead, they intend to rent the house to family members. The client confirmed that she would not need the firm's assistance with this.

The firm's bank details were provided to the client. She was advised that upon completion, there may be funds due back to her.

The client was advised that it is the policy of the firm to request a payment on account at the start of all new matters of £400. This allows us to cover general disbursements such as property search fees. The monies paid on account will be taken into consideration in the final completion statement when the matter has concluded.

We discussed whether they would be having their own survey/valuation carried out on the property. I advised that she attain a survey of the property which focuses on structural issues, given that the Property is 40 years old.

The clients are cash buyers and will not require a mortgage. The purchase is being funded by profits saved from their businesses. The client was advised that she would need to provide evidence of where the money has come from. The client explained the money was in a savings account and she can provide bank statements for the last six months. The client confirmed she had never been made bankrupt or the subject of an arrangement with creditors to consolidate debts, and that she was not aware of any circumstances in which this is likely to happen.

We discussed whether they currently have a will. The clients do not and would like more information from us on making a will. Referral to the wills department to be made as a next step.

Advice to the client regarding the conveyancing process
I explained the following to the client:
*   Upon instructing us, we ask that payment is made on account to commission the relevant property searches at the earliest opportunity. Thereafter, the seller's solicitors will prepare a draft contract and we will investigate the title.
*   The full conveyancing process, including searches, raising enquiries, report on title, exchange and completion.
*   Buildings insurance will need to be put in place for the exchange of contracts.
*   She would need to provide us with the deposit, which is normally 10% of the purchase price before exchange. We will prepare a draft completion statement at this stage showing the full amount required to complete the purchase.

On the day of completion, we will arrange to send the balance of purchase funds to the seller's solicitors, and as soon as they receive the same they will release the keys. We will confirm when this has taken place.

We are unable to give an indication of exactly what time this will be as this depends on the electronic banking system. After completion, we will register ownership at the Land Registry.

Next steps
The clients must do the following before work can commence:
- Provide proof of current address.
- Mr Brooks must attend the offices to have his ID certified and sign the retainer.
- Make a payment of £400 initially on account of costs.

Once the client has completed the above steps, the firm will write to Slattery Solicitors and the estate agents to confirm we are representing Mr and Mrs Brooks. I will also make a referral to the wills department.

Attachment 2

Suspicious client/matter report form

REPORT FORM: STRICTLY CONFIDENTIAL
Before completing this form, speak first to the money laundering officer. Great care must be taken to ensure that this form is not seen by the client at any time and it must not be stored on the matter file.

Client

(Mr) (Mrs) (Miss) (Ms) (Other)	**Forenames**: Daisy	
Surname: Brooks	**Alias or previous name**: unknown	
Phone (day): 07765876115	**Evening**:	**Mobile**:
Address: 42 Orchard Crescent, Weston		
Postcode: NG24 7DG	**Email**: ddbrooks@gmail.com	
Date and place of birth, if known: unknown	**NI no. if known**: unknown	

Circumstances

Source of client: New client who has come to us after seeing advertising.
Nature of instructions: Conveyancing matter
Reason for report (attach confidential memo if necessary): Please see Attendance note. Concerns arose following receipt of £21,000 from Martha Willis for the Brooks case. During the meeting Mrs Brooks did not mention that a Martha Willis would be paying, and the sum credited far exceeds the 10% deposit and our costs. Client ID has been obtained for Mrs Brooks but not her husband. He is jointly purchasing the property. Mrs Brooks claims to own many different businesses. Mrs Brooks emailed to ask that I return some of the money to her bank account. I am concerned that this could be an attempt at placement.

Signed: Alexander Thomas (Partner)
Date: 19.01.202#
Money Laundering Reporting Officer (MLRO)
MLRO Date Received: 19.01.202#
Date of report to National Crime Agency: 19.01.202#

* * *

> ### SQE1 Functional legal knowledge link
>
> If you need to revise your knowledge of money laundering, see **Revise SQE: Ethics and Professional Conduct**.
>
> The conveyancing process is in stages including pre-exchange, exchange of contracts, completion and post completion. If you need to revise your knowledge of the conveyancing process, see **Revise SQE: Property Law and Practice**.

STEP 1 ESTABLISH THE RELEVANT CONTENT THAT MUST BE INCLUDED

When communicating with a client, you need to ensure that you are including relevant facts and accurately outlining the legal issues. Your aim is to help the client make an informed decision. To achieve this, in some circumstances you will need to outline different options for the client and give your advice on which option would best meet the client's goals.

Assessment technique

While you read through the question, make a note of the key legal and/or procedural points you feel you must communicate to your client. Remember that you do not have the highlighting function in the assessment, so it may be easier to make a written note, or copy and paste key content onto your electronic document. Remember that you can only copy by pressing CTRL+C on your keyboard in the SQE2 assessment.

HAVE A GO

Try to pick out the relevant content from question 1.
1. At this initial stage, focus on defining the problem.
2. Remember that you should only select content that is relevant and will assist you in providing advice on what you have been specifically told to discuss.

The client in question 1 is a new client who is instructing the firm in relation to conveyancing. We therefore need to consider what the SRA requires solicitors to do when receiving instructions from a new client: all firms must provide information about their services at the point a new client instructs the firm. The challenge in this question is to write about standard client care matters which have been omitted from the original letter, but also manage the communication so that the partner does not commit any direct or indirect offence.

The initial client care letter should be clear, easy to understand and contain the right information. This should reduce potential client complaints as the client will have a document that clearly sets out what they should expect from their solicitor. This includes providing information on the likely cost involved in the case, and how to complain if things go wrong. The Code of Conduct for Solicitors, RELs and RFLs link box below explains more about the requirements for a client care letter, and you can assume that the client care letter sent by the partner in question 1 covered these points.

Code of Conduct for Solicitors, RELs and RFLs link

The SRA has issued specific guidance for law professionals to help solicitors understand their obligations for the client care letter and how to comply with them (see the SRA website). Being clear on costs at the outset in your client care letter, and as the matter progresses, can help prevent complaints to the Legal Ombudsman. Per rule 8.7 of the Code of Conduct for Solicitors, RELs and RFLs, you should ensure that clients receive the best possible information about how their matter will be priced and, both at the time of engagement and when appropriate as their matter progresses, about the likely overall cost of the matter and any costs incurred.

You also need to ensure, per rule 8.3 of the Code of Conduct for Solicitors, RELs and RFLs, that clients are informed in writing at the time of engagement about: their right to complain to you about your services and your charges; how a complaint can be made and to whom; any right they have to make a complaint to the Legal Ombudsman; and when they can make any such complaint.

The guidance suggests the following should be included in any client care letter:
- a clear explanation of the agreed work
- confirmation of what is and is not included in this work
- any next steps, including a clear explanation of the actions required from the client and where they can get further information if they need it
- a cost breakdown and explanation of any potential additional costs (this could include the searches)
- the likely timescales for the agreed work
- details of a named contact and how to get in touch if they have further queries
- how a client can complain if things go wrong.

Let's look at the key legal points for this question.

➡Key legal points: question 1

Turn to page 26 for the key legal points and provisions for committing direct and indirect offences in this area. Defences are available for indirect offences, which will be discussed in the Commentary to sample answer 1 on page 104.

We also need to consider the potential money laundering issues in this question. Conveyancing is an area of law that places law firms at a higher risk of money laundering. To avoid this risk, solicitors must adhere to the Money Laundering Regulations 2017 and the Proceeds of Crime Act 2002. The legislation requires solicitors to perform thorough checks to authenticate the identity, proof of address and source of funds of individuals involved in property transactions.

There are three key stages to money laundering:
1. **Placement**: criminal proceeds are introduced into the financial system. Proceeds can be introduced by being deposited as cash, or used to buy financial instruments, or directed through businesses, or used to buy high-value assets in less strictly regulated industries.
2. **Layering**: the source of the money is concealed by creating a layer of financial transactions to hide the original source.
3. **Integration**: money is moved into the general economy, making it appear to be legally earnt money.

> ### SQE 1 Functioning legal knowledge link
>
> If you need to revise your knowledge of money laundering, see **Revise SQE: Ethics and Professional Conduct**.
>
> Also, the Law Society has published an Anti-Money Laundering Obligations leaflet. This highlights some money laundering 'red flags' which solicitors should pay attention to.
>
> They include:
>
> - secretive clients
> - clients established or transacting business in 'high-risk' jurisdictions or 'high-risk' sectors
> - complex transactions with no apparent economic or legal purpose
> - unexplained cross-border elements in the transaction
> - large payments from private funds or payments from many individuals or sources
> - unusual pattern of transactions, eg an unusually rapid sale after purchasing a property, an unusual valuation, or a rapid change in client–solicitor instructions
> - changes to the solicitor's business relationship with long-standing clients, eg a transaction which falls outside the client's usual sector or a higher-than-usual value of the transaction
> - negative press surrounding the client.
>
> The SRA is responsible for managing compliance with these regulations. Should any solicitor fail to comply with the Money Laundering Regulations, the SRA may pursue disciplinary proceedings.

Let's apply those 'red flags' to question 1:

- There has been a larger than required payment from an individual who is not the client.
- The firm does not have evidence of where those private funds have come from.
- The client has been quite secretive. She had not disclosed that Martha Willis would be paying the deposit and legal fees, despite meeting the solicitor on the same day that payment was made.

Overall, it is reasonable that the partner has concerns and has reported them to the money laundering officer.

> ## ➥Key legal points: question 1
>
> There are ethical and professional conduct issues that are raised in the email. The firm now has £21,000 in a client account which was paid by an unknown third party, and Mrs Brooks is requesting money to be transferred to her via BACS.
>
> ### Can the firm return the money?
>
> The firm cannot just return the money at this stage. To do so would constitute 'tipping off', which is an indirect offence under s 333A of the Proceeds of Crime Act 2002. Regardless of whether or not the client is trying to launder money, the law firm will have to be careful. Returning the money would arguably amount to a breach of the SRA Accounts Rule 3.3, which states that law firms must not use the client account to provide banking facilities for clients.
>
> ### Can the firm tell Mrs Brooks about their concerns?
>
> No, Mrs Brooks must not be told that the firm suspects she is trying to launder money as this would also constitute 'tipping off'.

STEP 2 STRUCTURE YOUR RESPONSE IN A LOGICAL WAY

It is important to consider how to sequence your letter. Your letter should guide the reader through the facts, the relevant law and advice. If your structure is successful, the client should reach the conclusions you intended by the end of the letter. The Assessment technique box below contains a suggested structure for you to follow.

Assessment technique

1. Introduction paragraph

Start your first paragraph by linking back to the initial communication with the reader. For example:

- If you are writing following a face-to-face meeting or a telephone call, state this.
- If you are writing for the first time to the other side to litigation or the other side to the client's transaction, outline who you are acting for and who you understand they are acting for.

It is important that you do not start your letter by presenting your conclusions and advice. If you do so, a client will probably stop reading and not absorb all the information they need.

2. Background paragraph

Set out the relevant facts you have identified in **Step 1** (see page 96), as you will be basing your legal advice on this information. Clients sometimes neglect to provide all the information, and this can sometimes result in solicitors providing incorrect advice. It is therefore important that you set out the basis on which you are giving that advice. The onus is then on the client to correct any inaccuracies.

3. The law, advice and options paragraphs

Now set out the relevant law, your advice and the options available to the client. You might need to present this information in several separate paragraphs. Aim to deal with one topic per paragraph, to ensure the letter flows.

4. Next steps paragraph

You should then set out the next steps for this matter. This could include what you (the solicitor) will be doing next, and/or what the client should do next to progress the case. You might need the client to provide you with evidence or instructions.

5. Closing paragraph

This should act as a conclusion to your letter. It is usually good practice to conclude by reminding the client that they should contact you if they have any queries.

If you find it difficult to structure your letter, it might be helpful for you to include headings as a guide. Before you read the assessment question, set out a draft outline of the letter including the headings shown in the Assessment technique box above. Then when you have read the question, you can quickly input relevant information under each heading. Once you have created an initial draft, you can then formalise the letter. If you follow this advice, you are less likely to include content in an illogical place. For example, if you mention facts under the next steps heading, you should easily identify that you are not following a logical structure. You can remove these headings once you have finished your letter, or keep them in if you feel they are appropriate.

Headings can often be useful for a recipient to quickly identify specific parts of a letter they wish to read. For example, your busy supervisor who is reviewing your file may skip to the advice and next steps paragraphs to find out what stage the case is at, rather than read every detail of the letter.

HAVE A GO

Try to structure your letter following the advice in the Assessment technique box on page 99. Do bear in mind however that this is only a sample, and you should adjust this strategy to suit yourself. Remember that if you have prepared and practised a structure in advance, you are more likely to be successful in the assessment.

STEP 3 ENSURE THAT THE STYLE AND LANGUAGE OF THE LETTER IS APPROPRIATE FOR THE READER

Why is the identity of the reader relevant to style and language?

Every solicitor will have their own style of writing, but you must ensure your style is appropriate for your reader. Before you start drafting your letter, consider who the reader is. As mentioned in the introductory part of this chapter, for the SQE2 legal writing assessment we know the reader will either be:
- a client
- a third party
- the other side to litigation or to a client transaction, or
- a partner within your firm's organisation.

Assessment technique

Take time to think about who the reader is and what you want to achieve from that communication. Your style of writing will need to adapt to whatever suits that recipient. For example:
- A letter to a client is likely to be informative, and written in plain English without unnecessary legal jargon.
- A letter to the other side in a litigation matter will include specific legal terminology. It is likely to avoid disclosing unnecessary information which may hurt your client's case.
- If the client is a business, they will probably have previous experience of dealing with solicitors, such as renting business premises or negotiating contracts. You might not need to explain the law in as much detail as you would to an individual client, because the business client will be more familiar with solicitors' letters.
- If you are writing to an opposing law firm or litigant in person, you will need to be professional and persuasive.

How has technology impacted style and language?

Many of us rely on the spellcheck and synonym tools in Microsoft Word. It is easy to slip into the habit of trusting the computer to tell us if our writing does not make sense. When that help is removed, many people struggle with spelling, grammatical errors and understanding the meaning of particular words.

This technology will not be available to you in an SQE2 assessment. The onus will be on you to ensure you can write an appropriate letter.

Bad style and language habits to avoid in a legal letter

Writing lengthy sentences
When writing in time-pressured conditions, it is easy to include as much information on a page as possible, without considering how to express that information and how you expect others to read it.

Make sure that your sentences have appropriate punctuation so that the reader knows when to pause and take a breath. This will improve the digestibility of your letter. Lengthy sentences could make the reader lose sight of the point you are trying to make. It is poor practice for a typed sentence to be more than three lines long without any punctuation.

Being repetitive

You have limited time in the assessment to write your letter. It is therefore very important that you avoid making the same point more than once.

Using redundant words

Try to be concise when writing, and avoid using redundant words or phrases that do not bring any value to your letter. Where possible, avoid using phrases of two or more words when one will do.

Let's take this basic sentence as an example:

That is actually correct.

The word 'actually' is redundant and can be removed.

Using unfamiliar words in the wrong context

You might be tempted to use complex, unfamiliar words rather than simpler alternatives, to demonstrate your wide vocabulary and make your writing appear more formal. Unfortunately, using unfamiliar words in the wrong context might affect the accuracy of your letter and the clarity of your expression. Always check that you have a correct understanding of any new/unfamiliar words before you use them.

Look at this sentence as an example:

There are red flags suggesting money laundering is taking place.

If we select synonyms for the word 'suggesting', we can change the sentence as follows:
a.   *There are red flags <u>advising</u> money laundering is taking place.*
b.   *There are red flags <u>indicating</u> money laundering is taking place.*
c.   *There are red flags <u>hinting</u> money laundering is taking place.*
d.   *There are red flags <u>advocating</u> money laundering is taking place.*

However, note that only suggested sentence c makes sense in the context of the original sentence. Sentences a, b and d are not precise, and slightly change the meaning.

Using an inappropriate tense

Whether you use passive or active tense depends on the type of writing that you are working on. The active tense is often a more effective way to communicate ideas, although in certain circumstances the passive tense is necessary.

The active tense is where the subject is performing an action:

Mrs Daisy Brooks is requesting the return of funds.

The passive tense is where the action is the focus and the verb acts upon the subject:

The return of funds is requested by Mrs Daisy Brooks.

Using incorrect grammar, punctuation and spelling

You will not lose marks for spelling mistakes that do not affect the legal accuracy, clarity and/or certainty of the written text, or which would be flagged by spellcheck functionality. However, if most of your work is spelt incorrectly and has missing words, this will affect the impression created by your letter. Make sure you proofread your work before the end of the assessment.

Table 3.1 provides a reminder of punctuation symbols and when to use them.

Table 3.1 Punctuation symbols

Punctuation symbol	How to use the symbol
;	A semi-colon can be used in lists and to separate related clauses.
:	A colon is used when introducing a list or when following a sentence with an explanation.
.	A full stop ends a sentence.
,	A comma is used as a pause between parts of a sentence.
'	An apostrophe can indicate: • possession or ownership – the client's goal, or • a letter has been omitted – it's (instead of it is). Note that apostrophes are not required when indicating a plural: *I met the clients.*

Using incorrect salutations and endings

The correct salutations and endings depend on the recipient of the letter.

For a legal letter to an individual client:
• Use the salutation 'Dear Mrs Brooks'.
• If you know the individual well, it may be appropriate to use the client's first name, 'Dear Daisy'.
• Do not use the salutation 'Dear Daisy Brooks'.
• The letter should end with 'Yours sincerely' and the sender's individual signature.

For a legal letter to a company:
• Use the salutation 'Dear Sirs', regardless of whether you are writing to an individual of any gender at the company.
• End the legal letter with 'Yours faithfully' and the name of the firm.
• The letter should be signed in the firm's name and not the individual sender.

Attachments and enclosures
• For a legal letter, it is appropriate to say that any additional documents are enclosed.
• For emails, you should say that any additional documents are attached.

HAVE A GO

Practise your writing in a style that is appropriate for the reader of the letter. Determine whether you are writing the letter as an individual or on behalf of the company, and ensure you use the correct salutation and ending.

■ YOUR TURN

Have a go now at writing a legal letter in answer to question 1.
- Remember the stepped approach on pages 96–102.
- Refer to the structured approach in the SRA's assessment criteria on page 89.
- It will also be helpful for you to refer to the SRA website about what must be included in a client care letter.
- Timings are important: you will have 30 minutes in the assessment to prepare and write your answer. Use this as an opportunity to practise your time management skills by timing yourself.

EVALUATING YOUR ANSWER

Once you have attempted writing the letter, mark it yourself against the SQE2 legal writing assessment criteria. Do you think your attempt met the threshold standard?

Now compare your attempt with the following sample answers. A circled number indicates that commentary is provided for this part of the answer. The commentary will explain whether or not the sample is likely to meet the SQE2 standard threshold.

■ SAMPLE ANSWER 1 TO QUESTION 1

Your reference:
Our reference: Brooks/BR28L ❶

Mr and Mrs Brooks
42 Orchard Crescent
Weston
NG24 7DG

19 January 202#

Dear Mr and Mrs Brooks ❷

Purchase of 28 Lakeview Way, Nottingham, NG5 8PL at a price of £120,000 ❸

I write further to the letter dated 18 January 202# where we confirmed some important details about how we propose to provide our services. In addition to that letter, I write to confirm your legal position as individuals purchasing a property together and what identification documents we need to progress your matter. ❹

You have instructed us that the above named property is being purchased by you both jointly. ❺

I must explain that by acting for both of you, there is no duty to keep information that either of you has provided to us confidential from the other joint client. This means that information that either one of you gives to us must be capable of being disclosed to the other. If one of you supplies information but does not wish us to share it with the other joint client and it would be relevant to their involvement in this transaction, I may have to stop acting for you both in this matter. ❻

As a result of the property being purchased jointly, I must identify each of you to comply with government controls on money laundering, which requires solicitors to identify every client that we act for. ❼

I can confirm that we have photographic identification for Mrs Brooks, but we still require this for Mr Brooks. Unfortunately, I cannot accept the faded picture of Mr Brooks' passport received via email on the evening of 18 January 202#. I will require Mr Brooks to attend the offices with his in-date passport or photo driving licence so that we can verify his identity. ⑧

We also need to verify your current address. Please provide us with either a copy of a recent utility bill, council tax bill or bank statement (not more than three months old) which confirms your address.

Therefore, for work to start on the above matter, please could you provide us with sight of Mr Brooks' passport or photo driving licence, and evidence of the address for both of you. ⑨

In our previous letter you were provided with a retainer. To avoid any misunderstandings between us as to what we are doing for you and on what terms, if you have not done so already please read and sign the retainer, and then return it to us. Please keep the other copy in a safe place to consult in future if required. If you require any further information, have any queries or need advice on any aspect of the above matter, please do not hesitate to contact me. ⑩

Yours sincerely ⑪

Alexander Thomas (Partner)

COMMENTARY

❶ It is important to include references where possible. This enables the correspondence to be allocated to the correct file at the firm quickly and efficiently. Here, the candidate has correctly used the reference included in Attachment 1, the attendance note.

❷ The email from the partner confirmed that Mrs Brooks and her husband were purchasing the property together. It is therefore appropriate for the letter to be addressed to both.

❸ This is an appropriate subject heading for the letter, which clearly identifies the matter that the candidate is acting upon.

❹ This is a good opening paragraph which refers to the last meeting with the client and adheres to point 1 in the suggested structure provided in our Assessment technique box on page 99.

❺ This sets out the instruction received about how the property will be held. Further detail has not been added because this will have been already included by the client care letter sent the day prior. It is important that factual background is referred to in legal letters, because you are basing your advice on those instructions. If any facts are recorded inaccurately, this could lead to incorrect advice and professional conduct issues. By including this information in the letter, the candidate is giving the client an opportunity to correct anything that is inaccurate. This adheres to point 2 in the suggested structure provided in our Assessment technique box on page 99.

❻ This paragraph is particularly relevant because the property is being purchased by Mr and Mrs Brooks. It is important to outline the solicitor's duty to act in the best interests of both clients and outline the parameters of that work. This information has been communicated in a sensitive manner.

❼ Identifying clients is particularly important for conveyancing. A conveyancing solicitor must consider the *Land Registry Practice Guide 67 Evidence of identity*, the requirements of Land Registry forms which require confirmation of identity (this includes applications to change the register) and the identification requirements of the Council of Mortgage Lenders. This identity check must be completed. The paragraph does not constitute 'tipping off' because there is no suggestion that Mrs Brooks is attempting to launder money; instead, the letter is setting out the firm's policy, and the candidate demonstrates a correct application of the law.

8 Solicitors must take a copy of the original identification document and certify that they have seen the original document. Without doing so, matters should not progress, and this adheres to point 3 in the suggested structure provided in our Assessment technique box on page 99.

9 It is clearly explained that no further work will be completed until the client has completed the next steps. Those steps are easy for the client to identify. This adheres to point 4 in the suggested structure provided in our Assessment technique box on page 99.

10 This is an appropriate concluding paragraph. It reminds the client to contact the solicitor if any queries arise, and asks the client to sign the retainer, as mentioned in the email from the partner. This ensures that everyone is clear on the scope of the work agreed, and adheres to point 5 in the suggested structure provided in our Assessment technique box on page 99.

11 'Yours sincerely' is the correct sign-off because the letter is being written by a solicitor to an individual client.

Does this answer meet the threshold?

This letter includes the relevant facts from the attendance note. It also highlights what the firm needs from the client to proceed with the property purchase. There is a logical structure to the letter with content that is client-focused. Clear and precise language has been used that is appropriate, and the letter addresses professional conduct issues without 'tipping off' the client about the firm's suspicions of money laundering. It is therefore likely that this letter is competent to reach the SQE2 assessment criteria.

Now let's consider the second sample answer to question 1.

■ SAMPLE ANSWER 2 TO QUESTION 1

Your ref:
Our ref: Brooks/BR28L

Miss D Brooks, **1**
28 Lakeview Way,
Nottingham,
NG5 8PL

20 January **2**

Hi Daisey Brooks **3**

House purchase **4**

I can confirm have received a payment on your account for £21,000. I understand this was paid by your cousin Martha Willis. I am not sure whether you are aware or not, but this payment far exceeds our costs and the 10% house deposit. **5**

It was fab meeting you the other day! I am thrilled you decided to instruct us. It is so exciting have found a new home for yourself and your husband. **6**

All in all, its quite concerning Daisy. I have had no choice but to report you to our money laundering officer. I know you have requested some of the money back but I cant do that until our money laundering officer gives me the green light. **7**

Im not sure how long it will all take but if there is no issue, I am sure it will be resolved quickly! **8**

In the interim I have attached out standard terms an conditions AGAIN. **9**

These terms and conditions include information about our fees and how you can pay any outstanding moneys owed to ourselves. They also detail our complaints procedure (not that you need to know about that ☺). **10**

If you have any questions do not hesitate to contact the firm and speak to the money laundering officer. **11**

Yours faithfully **12**

Partner

COMMENTARY

1 There are three problems with this address:
- The client is married and introduced herself as 'Mrs' Brooks, therefore this title should be used.
- It is not necessary to include commas in an address.
- Most importantly, this is the incorrect address: it is the address of the property being purchased. This is a substantial professional conduct issue.

2 The full date has not been included. It is important that law firms have clear records of when work was completed, and the year is missing on this letter. You should include the date given on the question in your SQE2 legal writing assessment.

3 There are four style and language inaccuracies with this salutation:
- Daisy is spelt incorrectly. Whilst this is a small spelling mistake, it does not inspire trust and confidence from a client when a solicitor cannot spell their name correctly.
- Salutations should not include the client's full name. Instead, it would have been appropriate to write 'Dear Mrs Brooks' or 'Dear Daisy'.
- The salutation should say 'Dear'. Starting the letter with 'Hi' is too informal for a legal letter.
- The email from the partner confirmed that Mrs Brooks and her husband were purchasing the property together, so the letter should be addressed to both.

4 This subject heading between the salutation and the first paragraph is very brief. For letters to individual clients, the heading should describe the matter. From the heading in this answer, it is not clear whether this letter is about the clients purchasing 28 Lakeview Way or general advice about purchasing houses. A clearer heading would have been 'Your house purchase'.

Assessment technique

In property law transactions, it is good practice to include the property details in the heading and create a defined term. For example, an appropriate heading here would be 'Purchase of 28 Lakeview Way, Nottingham, NG5 8PL ("the Property")'.

5 This opening paragraph is not logically structured. The first sentence in a letter should put the letter into context, either by referring to the last correspondence or meeting you had with the client, or confirming the party you are representing if you have not previously met or corresponded with this client. The sentence also has a missing word ('I'), which affects its readability.

6 This paragraph is too informal. The use of exclamation marks is not appropriate, and this is not a logical place for this paragraph. The sentence also has a missing word ('you').

7 This paragraph would amount to 'tipping off' the client. An offence has therefore been committed under s 333A of the Proceeds of Crime Act 2002, because the client has been made aware of a disclosure. This is likely to prejudice any investigation that might be made, and is an offence that could be punishable by imprisonment and/or a fine. Whilst a defence is available under s 333D, the warning was not made to dissuade Mrs Brooks from engaging in money laundering, which means this defence will not be available to the candidate. This is a significant professional conduct issue.

There are also errors of punctuation in this paragraph. For example, there should be apostrophes in 'it's' and 'can't'. The paragraph also includes redundant words, such as 'all in all'.

8 An apostrophe is missing in 'I'm'. The sentence content is generally inappropriate, and the tone is too casual for a formal letter to a client (for reasons given in point 7), particularly the exclamation mark at the end of the sentence.

9 The sentence is missing a comma between 'interim' and 'I'. There are also typos, such as 'out' which should be 'our', and 'an' should be 'and'. Given the terms and conditions were only sent the day before, it would be more appropriate to remind the client to sign the document rather than send it again. The terminology is inappropriate: as this is a legal letter being sent by post rather than email, it should state that the terms and conditions are enclosed rather than attached. Finally, stating 'again' at the end of the sentence in capitals is inappropriate, and likely to be poorly received by the client.

10 It is helpful that a brief outline has been given about the terms and conditions, although this information will have already been provided in the initial client care letter. It is not necessary to repeat this information. For further information about what is included in a client care letter, see the Code of Conduct for Solicitors, RELs and RFLs link box on page 97. The candidate has made the client aware of the complaints procedure again, which is a Law Society requirement. However, including 'not that you need to know about that' is highly inappropriate and unprofessional. It is also unacceptable to use emojis in a legal letter.

11 It is not clear who Mrs Brooks should contact at the firm. Also, suggesting she contact the money laundering officer adds to the 'tipping off' issue mentioned in point 7 above.

12 This letter is being signed by an individual rather than a company. This means that it should state 'Yours sincerely' rather than 'Yours faithfully', so the candidate has failed to use appropriate language here.

Does this answer meet the threshold?

When assessed against the SQE2 legal writing assessment criteria, it is unlikely that this legal letter would meet the threshold standard. It contains irrelevant information and inappropriate, casual comments. The letter is not structured logically, and there is no clear introduction, background, application of law or advice. Instead, informal remarks have been mixed with legal information. The language is not entirely appropriate for a legal letter: phrases such as 'It was fab meeting you' and 'I am thrilled you decided to instruct us' are too informal. Additionally, the letter is littered with grammatical errors.

This letter's application of the law evidently amounts to 'tipping off' which, as mentioned above, means the law firm would have committed a criminal offence. This would create professional conduct issues for the firm and as such that part of the SQE2 threshold would not be satisfied. The candidate should not have disclosed that an investigation was being conducted. Also, if the seller of the property accidentally saw this letter and became aware of the firm's money laundering suspicions, it is possible that the sale would fall through. At this stage, the firm's suspicions are unsubstantiated and if the client is not attempting to launder money, this error by the firm could cost Mrs Brooks the purchase of the property.

The SRA can assess any of the areas on the SQE2 specification. Below is another example of how a different part of the specification, business organisations, rules and procedures, could arise in the context of SQE2 legal writing.

■ QUESTION 2

Email to candidate

From: Partner
Sent: 18 May 202#
To: Candidate
Subject: Claude Croghan

We have been instructed today by Claude Croghan, who is a director at a private company called Parker & Tyler Developers. The company specialises in building industrial estates on land and then renting out the units to smaller companies.

Usually, he instructs another firm of solicitors on behalf of the company, but he has come to us because he needs independent advice. He has explained that the company adopt the standard Model Articles for Private Companies Limited by Shares. The company has not amended the Model Articles.

His wife recently inherited a large plot of land from a distant relative. It is next to an industrial estate and is ripe for development. His wife has received letters from many property developers seeking to purchase the land, and amongst those letters is one from Parker & Tyler Developers.

Mr Croghan's wife does not share his surname and, as far as he is aware, Parker & Tyler Developers does not know that the owner of the land is his wife.

Although Mr Croghan's wife was not initially planning to sell the land, receiving such high offers has tempted her to do so and use the proceeds to pay off the mortgage on their jointly owned family home. If there is enough money left over from the sale, they also hope to take a trip to the Bahamas. Mr Croghan is worried that if Parker & Tyler Developers become aware that the land belongs to his wife, they will try to give a low offer and expect her to agree because he works for the company.

There is a board meeting at Parker & Tyler Developers in two days' time to discuss the purchase amongst other matters, and Mr Croghan needs advice quickly.

Unfortunately, I have been called to deal with another urgent matter, so I need you to write the letter for me. I have already prepared a separate initial client care letter with all the required information about the firm.

I would like you to write a letter to Mr Croghan explaining the following:
* **whether he has an interest in the land**
* **whether he needs to disclose the above information to the board**
* **if he does have an interest, the impact this would have on the board meeting.**

Mr Croghan is a company director and not a lawyer. He has some experience of legal correspondence, but I am unaware to what extent. Therefore, please make sure your letter is clear and includes a brief legal explanation where appropriate.

I attach an extract of the Model Articles for Private Companies Limited by Shares for you to consider (Attachment 1).

Thanks

Partner

Note to candidates:

Please assume that all issues in relation to client care/money laundering have already been dealt with by the partner.

Attachment 1

Contains public sector information licensed under the Open Government Licence v3.0.

SCHEDULE 1   Regulation 2

MODEL ARTICLES FOR PRIVATE COMPANIES LIMITED BY SHARES

PART 2
DIRECTORS
DIRECTORS' POWERS AND RESPONSIBILITIES

DECISION-MAKING BY DIRECTORS

14 Conflicts of interest

(1) If a proposed decision of the directors is concerned with an actual or proposed transaction or arrangement with the company in which a director is interested, that director is not to be counted as participating in the decision-making process for quorum or voting purposes.

(2) But if paragraph (3) applies, a director who is interested in an actual or proposed transaction or arrangement with the company is to be counted as participating in the decision-making process for quorum and voting purposes.

(3) This paragraph applies when—
 (a) the company by ordinary resolution disapplies the provision of the articles which would otherwise prevent a director from being counted as participating in the decision-making process;
 (b) the director's interest cannot reasonably be regarded as likely to give rise to a conflict of interest; or
 (c) the director's conflict of interest arises from a permitted cause.

(4) For the purposes of this article, the following are permitted causes—
 (a) a guarantee given, or to be given, by or to a director in respect of an obligation incurred by or on behalf of the company or any of its subsidiaries;
 (b) subscription, or an agreement to subscribe, for shares or other securities of the company or any of its subsidiaries, or to underwrite, sub-underwrite, or guarantee subscription for any such shares or securities; and
 (c) arrangements pursuant to which benefits are made available to employees and directors or former employees and directors of the company or any of its subsidiaries which do not provide special benefits for directors or former directors.

(5) For the purposes of this article, references to proposed decisions and decision-making processes include any directors' meeting or part of a directors' meeting.

(6) Subject to paragraph (7), if a question arises at a meeting of directors or of a committee of directors as to the right of a director to participate in the meeting (or part of the meeting) for voting or quorum purposes, the question may, before the conclusion of the meeting, be referred to the chairman whose ruling in relation to any director other than the chairman is to be final and conclusive.

(7) If any question as to the right to participate in the meeting (or part of the meeting) should arise in respect of the chairman, the question is to be decided by a decision of the directors at that meeting, for which purpose the chairman is not to be counted as participating in the meeting (or that part of the meeting) for voting or quorum purposes.

15   Records of decisions to be kept

The directors must ensure that the company keeps a record, in writing, for at least ten years from the date of the decision recorded, of every unanimous or majority decision taken by the directors.

* * *

■ YOUR TURN

Have a go at writing a legal letter in response to question 2.
- Remember the stepped approach on pages 96–102.
- Make sure you refer to the structured approach in the SRA's assessment criteria on page 89.
- Ensure you provide the advice to the correct client, ie Mr Croghan, and not Parker & Tyler Developers.
- Timings are important: you will have 30 minutes in the assessment to prepare and write your answer. Use this as an opportunity to practise your time management skills by timing yourself.

SQE1 Functioning legal knowledge link

If you need to revise the topic of conflicting interests, see chapter 3 of **Revise SQE: Business Law and Practice**.

EVALUATING YOUR ANSWER

Once you have attempted to write a letter, mark it yourself against the SQE2 legal writing assessment criteria. Do you think your attempt met the threshold?

Now compare your attempt with the 'Key legal points' box and two sample answers below. A circled number indicates that commentary is provided for this part of the answer. The commentary will explain whether or not the sample answer is likely to meet the SQE2 standard threshold.

➡Key legal points: question 2

The issue raised in question 2 is whether or not the director has a conflict of interests. There is a potential conflict, and probably an actual conflict, between the director's self-interest which in this case is to receive as much as possible for the land and the director's fiduciary duties which is owed to the company. The company in this case will want to further its own interests by paying as little as possible for the land.

Section 177(1) of the Companies Act 2006 imposes a duty on any director to declare the nature and extent of an interest to the other directors if they are in any way, directly or indirectly, interested in a proposed transaction or arrangement with the company.

The legal owner of the land is the director's wife, so this means Mr Croghan will not have a direct interest. However, the director does have an indirect interest in the transaction because he will benefit from the mortgage being paid off his jointly owned home. He will also want his wife to sell the land for as high a price as possible. This will conflict with the company's aim to buy the property for as low a price as possible.

As per s 177(4) of the Companies Act 2006, the director will need to make the declaration of the nature and extent of his interest before the company enters into the transaction.

Under s 177(2) of the Companies Act 2006, he can make this declaration:
- at a meeting of the directors; or
- by notice to the directors in accordance with s 184 of the Companies Act 2006 (notice in writing); or
- in accordance with s 185 of the Companies Act 2006 (general notice).

There are exceptions where a director does not need to declare an interest, which include:
- Section 177(5) of the Companies Act 2006 – if the director is not aware of the transaction or arrangement in question. For this purpose, a director is treated as being aware of matters that he ought reasonably to be aware of.
- Section 177(6) of the Companies Act 2006 – (a) if it cannot reasonably be regarded as likely to give rise to a conflict of interest; (b) if, or to the extent that, the other directors are already aware of it (and for this purpose the other directors are treated as aware of anything of which they ought reasonably to be aware); or (c) if, or to the extent that, it concerns terms of his service contract that have been or are to be considered (i) by a meeting of the directors, or (ii) by a committee of the directors appointed for the purpose under the company's constitution.

None of the exceptions apply in question 2.

Article 14 of the Model Articles states that if a proposed decision of the directors is concerned with an actual or proposed transaction with the company in which the director is interested, then that director cannot vote, nor can they count in the quorum at the board meeting.

Exceptions to art 14 are set out in art 14(2). This states that if art 14(3) applies, the director can count in the quorum and can vote. Permitted causes are set out in art 14(4). The exceptions to art 14 are not applicable to question 2, therefore Mr Croghan will not be able to vote or be counted in the quorum.

■ SAMPLE ANSWER 1 TO QUESTION 2

[*The law firm's address and contact details*]

Mr Claude Croghan
[*client's address*]

18 May 202#

Dear Mr Croghan

Declaration of an indirect interest

I write further to our recent meeting on 18 May 202#. At the meeting you sought to confirm whether you needed to disclose to Parker & Tyler Developers ('the company') that the property they are interested in purchasing belongs to your wife. You explained that you believe the company is not aware that your wife owns the land. You would prefer to avoid making this disclosure because you believe the company will expect your wife to take a low offer because you work for the company. You explained that you and your wife hope to raise a substantial sum from the sale to pay off the mortgage on the family home. You explained that the board of directors were due to meet in two days to discuss this purchase. ❶

As a director of the company, the law states that you have a duty to declare the nature and extent of any direct or indirect interest that you may have in a proposed transaction or arrangement with the company. Although it is your wife who legally owns the land, you will have an indirect interest in the transaction because the proceeds of sale are being used for the benefit of paying off your mortgage on the family home. ❷

This means that you must declare that you have an indirect interest in the company's purchase of the land. Once you have made this declaration, you will not be able to vote on the transaction or be counted in the quorum at the board meeting. ❸

You can make this declaration one of three ways. You can either:
1.   give notice to the directors in writing;
2.   send a general notice; or
3.   make a declaration at a meeting of the directors. ❹

If you give notice in writing it must be sent to all the directors, by hard copy or an agreed electronic format. If you make the declaration by way of general notice, you must do this at a meeting of the directors, or ensure that it is brought up and read at the next meeting of the directors, after it is given to the directors of the company. To make a declaration at a meeting of the directors, the full board must be convened. This disclosure would need to be the first item on the agenda so that you can declare your interest before the company enters the transaction to purchase your wife's land.

On the basis that the board meeting is in two days, I would advise you to give notice to the directors in writing, ideally over email if that can be agreed, and make a declaration at the meeting of directors. ❺

If you make the declaration at the beginning of a board meeting, you should ensure that it is recorded in the board minutes to avoid any confusion or repercussions at a later stage. I have enclosed a precedent which you can amend and ask to be added to the board minutes. ❻

If you do not comply with the law by declaring your interest, you will be breaching your duty as a director. There could be various consequences, including claims or actions by the company against you. **7**

If you require any further information, have any queries, or need advice on any aspect of the above matter, please do not hesitate to contact me.

Yours sincerely

Partner

Enclosures: Board Minutes Precedent

COMMENTARY

1 This paragraph provides an overview of the issue and includes relevant facts. It is particularly important to outline who the company is, and why there may be a conflict of interest. It also shows the use of a defined term ('the company'), which means the company's name does not need to be repeated (see the Assessment technique box on page 106).

2 In this paragraph the candidate has avoided using legal jargon by instead commenting what 'the law states'. It is likely that as a company director Mr Croghan will be aware of the Companies Act 2006, but given he is a new client it is appropriate to avoid referring to specific legislation. Some legal terminology has been used such as 'indirect interest', but this has been explained.

3 Here the candidate confirms their advice, specifically that Mr Croghan must declare the interest, and concisely explains the impact of making the declaration as per art 14 of the Model Articles.

4 The advice provided here is clear and precise, and applies the law correctly. This is also an appropriate use of a list, with the correct use of semi-colons.

5 In these paragraphs, the candidate attempts to assist the client make a decision about how to make the declaration of interest. This is appropriate following the outline of the different options, as the client may need some direction on which method to choose.

6 Specific reference has been made to a document which is being enclosed. This has also been correctly referred to at the end of the letter. Inclusion of this document demonstrates the candidate's appreciation that the client's focus will be to protect his position and that to do so he would benefit from precedent wording being included in the board minutes. This shows an ability to exercise judgement to act in the client's best interests and avoid any future potential problems.

7 The paragraph explains the consequences of not declaring an interest, as a further action in the client's interest. It is only a brief mention, because the letter is rightly focused on the question raised in the email. Remember that there is limited time in the assessment, so you should only make fleeting mention of something that you have not been specifically asked to include.

Does this answer meet the threshold?

This sample answer is likely to be competent and meet the SQE2's standard threshold. It includes relevant facts, such as the client's wife owning the property, the client's indirect interest in the transaction and the need for disclosure before the board meeting. The letter has a logical structure: it starts with a reference to the recent meeting, explains the legal duty and implications, outlines options for making the declaration, and finally provides a clear recommendation. Each paragraph flows logically to the next.

The letter is focused on the client's situation and provides clear and practical advice on how to proceed. The style of writing is clear, precise and concise, and includes acceptable language which is appropriate. The law has been correctly applied, and the candidate both identifies future problems and attempts to resolve them with honesty and integrity. The letter comprehensively applies the law by detailing the methods of declaration and the urgency due to the upcoming board meeting.

Now let's consider the second sample answer to question 2.

■ SAMPLE ANSWER 2 TO QUESTION 2

[*The law firm's address and contact details*]

Mr Claude Croghan
[*client's address*]

18 May 202#

Dear Mr Croghan

Declaration ❶

You should make a declaration that you have an interest in the proposed transaction we discussed during our meeting on 18 May 202#. ❷

Section 177(1) Companies Act 2006 imposes a duty on any director who is in any way, directly or indirectly, interested in a proposed transaction or arrangement with the company to declare the nature and extent of that interest to the other directors. ❸

You do not fall within any of the exceptions in Section 177(5) and (6) of the companies Act 2006. ❹

If you do not declare an interest in the transaction this could lead to any of the following consequences:

a) A breach of common law rules or equitable principle because you owe a fiduciary duty to the company.
b) The company may rescind the contract with your wife.
c) Civil consequences under Section 178(1) of the Companies Act 2006.
d) Breach of contract your contract as a director.
e) Disqualification (under the articles).
f) Misrepresentation.
g) Conspiracy.
h) Conversion.
i) Fraud.
j) Action by the Financial Conduct Authority
k) An unfair prejudice petitions. ❺

If you require any further information, have any queries or need advice on any aspect of the above matter, please do not hesitate to contact me.

Kind regards ❻

Partner

COMMENTARY

1 This title is too short and is unclear. 'Declaration' could be in relation to any matter. This needs to be more specific.

2 Whilst it is good that the sentence refers to the initial meeting, the sentence is poorly structured. The letter dives straight into advice without explaining the factual background or why that is the correct advice. The advice is therefore not logically structured.

3 This is a very lengthy sentence, and there is no attempt to apply its contents to the facts of this matter. Unnecessary legal jargon has been included which is unlikely to be easily understood by the client.

4 This sentence does not make sense. It is not clear what is meant by exceptions, and the sentence includes legal jargon which is not explained. Reference to this legislation is unlikely to be helpful for Mr Croghan. Also note that the candidate has been inconsistent in not capitalising 'companies' in this paragraph, although it is capitalised in the previous paragraph.

5 This paragraph is problematic for many reasons:
- There is no explanation of these consequences of not making a declaration, and the reference to legislation will make little sense to the client.
- Some of the consequences are not relevant to the facts of this matter, which will be confusing for the client.
- The content in this paragraph is not what the partner instructed to be included in the letter.
- Whilst some consequences would correctly apply for this case, the list would probably create more confusion for the client than clarity.
- The punctuation is poor and inconsistent: commas are missing, and some but not all items in the list end with a full stop.

6 This is not a formal way to end a letter. The most appropriate and professional sign-off for a letter to a client in this situation would be 'Yours sincerely'.

Does this answer meet the threshold?

The letter does not include any of the relevant facts from the email. The letter starts with the conclusion, which is not a logical structure and may mean that the client does not read the whole letter. The letter is not focused on the issues it was intended to address by the partner, which means it is not client-focused. The commentary has highlighted certain problems with the letter which suggest that it does not meet the assessment requirement for clear, precise, concise and appropriate language.

There is no application of the relevant facts to the law, and only basic law is discussed. The letter does not attempt to apply the law to resolve any ethical and professional conduct issues. If anything, the letter is arguably unprofessional. Overall, the letter is unlikely to be competent and would probably fail to meet the SQE2 standard threshold.

■ KEY POINT CHECKLIST

This chapter has covered the following key points:
- The SQE2 assessment criteria for legal writing, applied in the context of professional conduct issues, including money laundering and a company director's conflict of interests.
- A suggested structure for approaching an SQE2 legal writing assessment.
- Sample answers that show what would be likely or unlikely to meet the SRA's Day One Solicitor competency standard.

■ SUMMARY AND REFLECTION

There are many steps to achieving success in the SQE2 legal writing assessment:
• Read all the information carefully, so that you will be able to cross-reference any necessary documents in your answer.
• Make a brief plan to include all the legal points that you want to raise. You could start by including headings that follow a logical structure, and then fitting those points into that structure. This will ensure that you do not miss any of the vital points and the letter is sequenced clearly. To help your self-reflection, review the commentaries in this chapter and note down any legal points that you might have missed in your own attempts to answer questions 1 and 2.
• Remember the assessment criteria. You need to show that you can apply the law and write in a professional manner. You will need to ensure that any advice provided to a client is clear and concise.
• Use language that is appropriate for your reader, to avoid being penalised in the assessment. When writing to clients, use clear language and avoid using legal jargon. When writing to the other side's solicitors, legal terminology will be expected. Practise writing letters to the different types of reader, so that you can adapt your writing style accordingly.

4

Legal drafting

◼ INTRODUCTION TO LEGAL DRAFTING

This chapter deals with the written skill of legal drafting. Whilst you may have some experience completing legal drafting in practice or during undergraduate study, this does not mean you are meeting the criteria set by the SRA. It is crucial to focus your revision on the SRA's expectations of a Day One Solicitor and how you will be examined in the SQE2 assessment.

This chapter explains what legal drafting is and why it is an important legal skill for a solicitor. It then explores how legal drafting is assessed under SQE2. Next, the chapter will consider the criteria you will be assessed against in the legal drafting SQE2 assessment. This will be followed by a detailed commentary of that assessment criteria.

Finally, this chapter will demonstrate a stepped approach to legal drafting in the context of a criminal litigation case study (question 1). We have provided you with two sample answers to scrutinise. Thereafter, you will have the opportunity to practise your own legal drafting skills in question 2, in the context of a business practice, and produce your own answer. Again, there will be two sample answers which you can use to help you reflect on your own answer.

WHAT IS LEGAL DRAFTING, AND WHY IS IT AN IMPORTANT SKILL FOR A SOLICITOR?

Legal drafting is the process of preparing legal documents that accurately reflect the legal requirements and intentions of the parties involved. It involves the creation of a variety of legal documents, such as contracts, wills, deeds and judgments, etc.

Legal drafting is an important skill for a solicitor for several reasons, as shown in Table 4.1.

In summary, legal drafting enables solicitors to create documents that are legally correct, clear, precise, concise and effective in protecting their clients' interests.

HOW IS LEGAL DRAFTING ASSESSED IN SQE2?

The SQE2 written centralised assessments take place over three half-days. You will be assessed on your legal drafting skills on each day:
- Day one – in the context of dispute resolution or criminal litigation.
- Day two – in the context of property practice or wills and intestacy, probate administration and practice.
- Day three – in the context of business organisations, rules and procedures.

In the assessment you will complete a 45-minute computer-based assessment that requires you, as a competent Day One Solicitor, to draft a legal document or parts of a legal document.

Table 4.1 The importance of developing excellent legal drafting skills

Values of good drafting	Why are these important?
Precision and clarity	Legal documents must be precise and clear to avoid any ambiguity or misunderstanding. A well-drafted document ensures that all parties understand their rights and obligations, which can prevent disputes.
Legal compliance	Drafting legal documents requires a thorough understanding of the law to ensure that the documents comply with current legal standards and requirements. This helps to safeguard the legal interests of the client and ensures that the documents are legally enforceable.
Risk management	Effective legal drafting helps in identifying and mitigating potential risks. By clearly outlining the terms and conditions, a solicitor can protect their client from future legal issues and liabilities.
Negotiation and advocacy	Drafting is often part of the negotiation process. A solicitor needs to draft documents that advocate for their client's best interests (SRA Principle 7) and are acceptable to other parties. This requires a solicitor to exercise care and skill in balancing assertiveness with diplomacy.
Professionalism	High-quality legal drafting reflects the professionalism and competence of the solicitor. It enhances the solicitor's reputation and can lead to better client satisfaction and retention.
Time- and cost-efficiency	Properly drafted legal documents can save time and costs in the long run by preventing legal disputes and the need for litigation. Clear and comprehensive documents minimise the likelihood of misinterpretation.

You will be provided with a memorandum in the form of an email from a partner, explaining the legal drafting that is required. You might be asked to draft from a precedent, or amend a document already drafted. You may also be required to draft a document without the benefit of any precedent or existing document.

As a solicitor, and depending on your area of practice, you may be required to draft a wide variety of legal documents. Table 4.2 lists some common types of document in the areas of law that SQE2 examines. Please note that we cannot know for certain whether you will be asked to draft any of these documents in the SQE2 assessment, and this is not an exhaustive list.

Drafting these documents requires:
• a thorough understanding of legal principles
• attention to detail
• the ability to tailor documents to the specific needs of clients.

Table 4.2 Common types of document in different areas of the law

Area of law examined by SQE2	Type of document to require drafting
Business	• Partnership agreement • Service agreement • Shareholder agreement • Articles of incorporation
Criminal practice	• Defence statement • Application to exclude evidence of a defendant's bad character • Bail appeal notice • Application for legal aid funding for a defendant • Application to exclude hearsay evidence
Dispute resolution	• Particulars of claim • Witness statement • Contract • Court orders • Settlement agreement
Property	• Lease agreement • Contract for sale • Deed • Transfer contract
Wills	• Deed of trust • Alterations and amendments to will • Estate planning

■ ASSESSMENT CRITERIA AND COMMENTARY

As you prepare your answer in the SQE2 assessment for legal drafting, remember that it will be judged against the following criteria:

SQE2 legal drafting assessment criteria

Skills assessment criteria

1. Use clear, precise, concise and acceptable language.
2. Structure the document appropriately and logically.

Application of law assessment criteria

3. Draft a document which is legally correct.
4. Draft a document which is legally comprehensive, identifying any ethical and professional conduct issues and exercising judgement to resolve them honestly and with integrity.

Let's look more closely at each point in these criteria, and explore the SRA's standard of competency as detailed in their performance indicators for SQE2 legal drafting.

SKILLS ASSESSMENT CRITERIA

1. Use clear, precise, concise and acceptable language

For a reminder of what clear, precise, concise and acceptable language means, please see Chapter 1, page 5.

When drafting, you should use an active voice. An active voice is usually easier to understand and is less ambiguous. If you need a reminder on the difference between active and passive voice, please review Chapter 3, page 101.

You will demonstrate **competence** if you:
- use understandable and simple language to convey facts and information effectively
- use suitably formal words and phrases
- use correct and necessary legal terminology
- are as concise as possible without compromising the quality of the answer.

You will **not** demonstrate **competence** if:
- your drafting is wordy, repetitive or confusing, and cannot be easily understood by the reader
- the meaning of the document is impossible to understand because it is too brief
- you use inappropriate language which is too informal
- you use unnecessary technical terms/legal jargon throughout.

2. Structure the document appropriately and logically

Structure is very important when drafting because it enhances readability, professionalism and completeness. A well-structured legal document minimises the risk of ambiguity or relevant points being missed.

You will demonstrate **competence** if the facts and information are set out in a methodical way.
- The focus, flow and direction of each paragraph should be clear.
- There should be appropriate signposts (such as headings) to guide the reader through the answer.
- The structure of the contents should help to achieve the purpose of the answer.

You will **not** demonstrate **competence** if your arrangements of facts or information are disjointed or confusing. This could occur if the structure of the answer is illogical. Structure is important when drafting, and you will not be competent if the content of your answer is not sequenced in a way that achieves its purpose.

APPLICATION OF LAW ASSESSMENT CRITERIA

3. Draft a document which is legally correct

You will demonstrate **competence** if you correctly identify and apply the relevant legal principles in accordance with the SQE2 assessment specification when drafting. The document must be legally effective, which means that it should contain all key information or the names of the relevant parties.

You will **not** demonstrate **competence** if you have not identified the correct legal principles or applied those principles when drafting, and consequently the document is not legally effective.

4. Draft a document which is legally comprehensive

You need to identify any ethical and professional conduct issues and exercise judgement to resolve them honestly and with integrity.

You will demonstrate **competence** if:
- your drafted document is sufficiently detailed in the context of the client's situation
- you have recognised ethical problems amongst the facts and legal issues included in the question, and can exercise effective judgement to address these problems in accordance with the SRA Principles and rules of professional conduct.

You will **not** demonstrate **competence** if:
- the drafting you have completed is not sufficiently detailed in the context of the factual and legal issues in the client's situation
- you fail to identify ethical issues or exercise effective judgement to address them according to the SRA Principles and rules of professional conduct.

◼ A STEPPED APPROACH TO LEGAL DRAFTING

Legal drafting can be broken down into three basic steps:
1. Establish the relevant content that must be included.
2. Structure the document in a logical way.
3. Ensure the writing style and language are appropriate for the drafted document.

Let's now work through question 1 and break down the steps to draft a legal document. This stepped approach will assist you to meet the SRA's assessment criteria, which is crucial to success in the SQE2 assessment. Question 1 focuses on criminal practice and a professional conduct issue: misleading the court (paragraph 1.4 of the Code of Conduct for Solicitors).

◼ QUESTION 1

Email to candidate

From: Partner
Sent: 20 February 202#
To: Candidate
Subject: Defendant Lynne Parsons – Case reference number: MG03064

You will recall that we are prosecuting the above-named defendant with criminal damage contrary to ss 1(1) and 4 of the Criminal Damage Act 1971.

I attended the first hearing on 15 February. As part of the Initial Details of the Prosecution Case (IDPC), we disclosed the previous convictions of the prosecution witness, Leah Flossie, and confirmed that there is no other unused material that might reasonably undermine our case or assist the defence case.

The defendant entered a not guilty plea, and the matter has been adjourned to 3 June for trial. We made the court and defence counsel aware at the hearing that we were intending to make an application to admit the defendant's bad character into evidence for the trial on 3 June.

Now the defendant has confirmed her plea, we are starting to prepare the case for trial. Part of that preparation includes drafting an application to admit the defendant's previous convictions into evidence at trial.

Please review the Memorandum of Conviction (Attachment 1) and Record of Interview (Attachment 2), and then draft a notice to introduce evidence of the defendant's bad character. I have attached a template for you to complete (Attachment 3).

Thanks

Partner

Note to candidates:

Attachment 2 is a partial extract and not the full document. A concise portion has been provided to accommodate the time constraints of this assessment.

Attachment 1

Extract from Memorandum of Conviction

MAGISTRATES' COURT

1.	CRIMINAL DAMAGE On 1/5/23 (Plea: Guilty) Criminal Damage Act 1971 S.1(1)	Fine 100.00 Compensation 36.00
2.	DRUNK AND DISORDERLY On 1/5/23 (Plea: Guilty) Criminal Justice Act 1967 S.91	Fine 20.00 Costs 25.00

____

MAGISTRATES' COURT

1.	ASSAULT OCCASIONING ACTUAL BODILY HARM an On 24/08/23 (Plea: Guilty) Offences Against The Person Act 1861 S.47	Community Order with unpaid work requirement (80 hours) Compensation 250.00
2.	CRIMINAL DAMAGE On 10/11/23 (Plea: Not Guilty) Criminal Damage Act 1971 S.4	Fine 100.00 Compensation 36.00

Attachment 2

Record of interview

Person interviewed: Lynne Parsons
Place of interview: Swan Police Station
Date of interview: 20 January 202#
Time commenced: 9.10
Time concluded: 9.38
Duration of interview: 28 minutes
Interviewing officer(s): DC 161 Rushby and PC 1280 Watkins
Tape reference no.: C0104/23
Other persons present: Defendant solicitor

Tape counter times	Person speaking	Text
0.00		Introduction and caution
01.20	Rushby	You were arrested this morning, on suspicion of Criminal Damage contrary to sections 1(1) and 4 of the Criminal Damage Act 1971 for an offence committed on 10 January 202#. Do you understand that?
	Parsons	Yes

| 01.35 | Rushby | Whilst in the police car, the PC told you that you had been named as being involved in the criminal damage to Neston's public house, and you replied, 'Sure, sure, if that's what you have been told it must have been me then.' Do you confirm or deny that statement? |
| | Parsons | I agree I said something like that, but I was being sarcastic obviously. Loads of people don't like me round here and have got it in for me. I know it was Leah Flossie who has told you it was me. She is a liar. She has had it in for me ever since I slept with her boyfriend. |

Attachment 3

Contains public sector information licensed under the Open Government Licence v3.0.

NOTICE TO INTRODUCE EVIDENCE OF A DEFENDANT'S
BAD CHARACTER
(Criminal Procedure Rules, rule 21.4(2))

Case details
Name of defendant:
Court:
Case reference number:
Charge(s):

This notice is given by [the prosecutor]
[. . . . . (name of co-defendant)]
I want to introduce evidence of the bad character of . . . .
. . . . (defendant's name) **on the following ground(s) in the Criminal Justice Act 2003:**
☐ **it is important explanatory evidence: s.101(1)(c).**
☐ **it is relevant to an important matter in issue between that defendant and the prosecution: s.101(1)(d).**
☐ **it has substantial probative value in relation to an important matter in issue between that defendant and a co-defendant: s.101(1)(e).**
☐ **it is evidence to correct a false impression given by that defendant: s.101(1)(f).**
☐ **that defendant has made an attack on another person's character: s.101(1)(g).**

<u>**How to use this form**</u>
1. **Complete the boxes above and give the details required in the boxes below.**
   If you use an electronic version of this form, the boxes will expand. If you use a paper version and need more space, you may attach extra sheets.
2. **Sign and date the completed form.**
3. **Send a copy of the completed form to:**
   (a) the court, and
   (b) each other party to the case.

<u>**Notes:**</u>
1. You must send this form so as to reach the recipients within the time prescribed by Criminal Procedure Rule 21.4(3) or (4). The court may extend that time limit, **but if you are late you must explain why**.

2. A party who objects to the introduction of the evidence must apply to the court under Criminal Procedure Rule 21.4(5) **not more than 14 days after service of this notice**.

---

1) **Facts of the misconduct.** If the misconduct is a previous conviction, explain whether you rely on (a) the fact of that conviction, or (b) the circumstances of that offence. If (b), set out the facts on which you rely.

---

2) **How you will prove those facts, if in dispute.** A party who objects to the introduction of the evidence must explain which, if any, of the facts set out above are in dispute. Explain in outline on what you will then rely to prove those facts, eg whether you rely on (a) a certificate of conviction, (b) another official record (and if so, which), or (c) other evidence (and if so, what).

---

3) **Reasons why the evidence is admissible.** Explain why the evidence is admissible, by reference to the provision(s) of the Criminal Justice Act 2003 on which you rely.

---

4) **Reasons for any extension of time required.** If this notice is served late, explain why.

Signed: . . . . **[prosecutor]**
[co-defendant / co-defendant's solicitor]

Date: . . . .

* * *

> ### ➦ Key legal points: question 1
>
> Criminal Procedure Rules 8.3(a) and 8.3(b) set out what needs to be included in the IDPC. Criminal Procedure Rule 8.3(b) states that in cases where Criminal Procedure Rule 8.3(a) does not apply, the IDPC must include:
> - a summary of the circumstances of the offence
> - any account given by the defendant in interview, whether contained in that summary or another document
> - any written witness statement or exhibit that the prosecutor then has available and considers material to plea, or to the allocation of the case for trial, or to sentence
> - the defendant's criminal record (if any), and
> - any available statement of the effect of the offence on a complainant, a complainant's family or others.
>
> Familiarise yourself with these documents in the event they are attached to the email from the partner.

STEP 1 ESTABLISH THE RELEVANT CONTENT THAT MUST BE INCLUDED

When drafting you should start by thinking about the purpose of the document. For example, is the intention to create a legally binding agreement, or prepare a court application?

Once you have established the purpose, you need to think about who is going to be using that document and how it is going to be used. For example, witnesses are often cross-examined in court on what has been written in their statement. It is therefore important when drafting an individual's statement that you use terminology the witness would use, and not exaggerate what they stated or change the style of expression. A good example is where a witness tells you in an interview that they were 'scared', and you wrote that down on the statement as they were 'terrified'. The words have different implications, and the witness could be accused of exaggerating or face scrutiny under cross-examination, when in fact it was a solicitor's drafting error.

You also need to think about what issues should be covered when drafting. Your document should address the relevant facts and any specific instructions you have received.

Try to think outside the box to foresee any issues your client has not envisaged. For example, if you are instructed to write a contract, your client may not have instructed you to add information about termination of that contract, thinking this will not be necessary. But it is your job to think about when the circumstance's termination may occur and safeguard your client's interests. Equally, you need to make sure the contract you produce is reasonable. It would not be appropriate to produce a contract that is solely in favour of your client.

Consider whether it is appropriate to use a precedent. As mentioned on page 118, you could be asked in the SQE2 assessment to draft from a precedent or amend one.

Drafting from a precedent

Precedents can take many different forms, and a law firm may have its own precedent letters, particularly client care letters. You will also find precedents online on legal search engines, such as Lexis+ and Practical Law.

When using a precedent, read it carefully before tailoring it to what you are drafting.

Amending a precedent

If you are asked to amend a precedent, you will need to determine what content is irrelevant and should be removed.

You might need to add to a precedent, so make sure that what you are writing is consistent with the remainder of the precedent. For example, if the precedent refers to the document as a 'Contract' in one sentence, it would not be appropriate for you to refer to it as an 'Agreement' in another.

Once you have finished making your amendments, check that the numbering of the clauses or sections is correct.

HAVE A GO

Try to pick out the relevant content that must be included from the question. Consider who you are acting for, and whether the question is asking you to draft from a precedent, amend a precedent or complete some free drafting.

It is important that you read through the instructions and attachments carefully to establish the relevant content.

Let's work through **Step 1** for question 1. In this question you are acting for the prosecution.

Code for Crown Prosecutors link

You should have identified in question 1 that you are acting for the crown prosecution service (CPS). The CPS should comply with the Code for Crown Prosecutors, which gives guidance to prosecutors on the general principles to be applied when making decisions about prosecutions.

Full details of the Code for Crown Prosecutors are available on their website: www.cps.gov.uk/publication/code-crown-prosecutors.

You have been given a precedent form to complete, which means you are amending a precedent. The purpose of the form is to introduce evidence of the defendant's bad character. In addition to the form, there are two attachments you need to consider.

➥ Key legal points: question 1

As per Rule 21.4(2) of the Criminal Procedure Rules, a prosecutor or co-defendant who wants to introduce such evidence must serve a notice on the court officer and any defendants.

If a notice is not given as required by Rule 21.4 of the Criminal Procedure Rules, the court may take the failure into account in exercising its powers to order costs under s 111(4) of the Criminal Justice Act 2003.

It is therefore your task to determine 'how' the prosecution can justify the inclusion of the defendant's bad character into court proceedings. To determine the 'how', you must be aware of s 101 of the Criminal Justice Act 2003.

Introduction of a defendant's bad character is governed by s 101 of the Criminal Justice Act 2003. In reference to question 1, previous convictions are deemed as bad character under s 98 of the Criminal Justice Act 2003.

There are seven gateways under s 101(1):

a) **All parties to the proceedings agree to the evidence being admissible.**
For this ground to apply, the prosecution and defence will need to agree that the bad character should apply. This section is not on the precedent because an application is not required where the parties agree. Thus, it is not relevant to question 1.

b) **The evidence is adduced by the defendant himself or is given in answer to a question asked by him in cross-examination and intended to elicit it.**
An example of this would be where the defendant referred to their previous convictions during a police interview or mentioned their previous convictions during cross-examination. Again, this section is not on the precedent because an application would not be required. Thus, it is not relevant to question 1.

c) **It is important explanatory evidence.**
Evidence is considered important explanatory evidence if the court would find it difficult or impossible to properly understand other evidence in the case without it, or the value of the evidence for understanding the case as a whole is substantial.

d) **It is relevant to an important matter in issue between the defendant and the prosecution.**
The matters in issue between the defendant and the prosecution include whether the defendant has a propensity either to commit offences of the kind with which he is charged or to be untruthful.

Consider whether the offence is of the same description as the one which the defendant is charged with. *R v Hanson* [2005] EWCA Crim 824 identifies three questions which should be considered:

i   Did the history of convictions establish a propensity to commit offences of the kind charged?
ii   Did that propensity make it more likely that the defendant committed the offence charged?
iii Was it unjust to rely on the convictions of the same description or category and, in any event, would the proceedings be unfair if they were admitted?

Applying *R v Hanson* [2005] to the scenario in question 1, having only one previous conviction for an offence of the same description or category as the one being charged is unlikely to show propensity.

e) **It has substantial probative value in relation to an important matter in issue between the defendant and a co-defendant.**
Only a co-defendant can apply under this section. 'Important matter' is defined as a matter of substantial importance in the context of the case. This could include evidence of propensity to commit an offence of that type, and evidence of propensity to be untruthful.

f) **It is evidence to correct a false impression given by the defendant.**
A defendant will have given a 'false impression' if they make an expression or implied assertion to the court that gives a false or misleading impression about themselves. Denying committing an offence will not amount to creating a false impression.

g) **The defendant has made an attack on another person's character.**
A defendant will have made an attack on another person's character if:
• They adduce evidence by attacking the other person's character.

- Defendant legal representation asks such questions in cross-examination that are intended or likely to elicit such evidence.
- Evidence is given of an attack on the character of another by the defendant on being questioned under caution, before charge, about the offence with which they are charged, or on being charged with the offence or officially informed that he might be prosecuted for it.

The prosecution will need to satisfy at least one of these gateways for a defendant's bad character to be introduced.

SQE 1 Functioning legal knowledge link

If you are unfamiliar with any of the above, we recommend you review the contents of *Revise SQE: Criminal Practice*.

STEP 2 STRUCTURE THE DOCUMENT IN A LOGICAL WAY

Determining the structure of your document depends heavily on what you have been asked to draft. We will explore the structure of question 1 in the Assessment technique box on page 129, but first let's review the structure of a very basic contractual agreement:

1. **Front cover**: this usually names the parties and gives a general description of the document, eg Agreement.
2. **Contents page**: this is more commonly used for lengthy documents.
3. **Commencement**: this part confirms who the parties are to the contract and mentions the date of contractual commencement.
4. **Recitals** (if applicable): a recital is usually used to outline background information or the intention of the contractual agreement. It could be utilised where the contract is a supplemental document and it is referring to the original, or it could be to safeguard against a different party denying a particular fact.
5. **Definitions**: this is where key terms will be defined.
6. **Conditions**: a conditions clause is relevant where certain things must be fulfilled before the contract becomes effective.
7. **Clauses reflecting agreement reached between the parties**: this is the key part of the agreement that discusses what has been agreed and the obligations and rights of the parties.
8. **Termination of contract**: this part discusses the right to terminate a contract.
9. **Technical provision**: this can include confidentiality clauses or non-competition clauses.
10. **Signatures, execution**: at the end of the document, the agreement should be signed and executed (this means that the signature has been witnessed).

SQE 1 Functioning legal knowledge link

If you are unfamiliar with any of the above headings, we recommend you review the contents of *Revise SQE: Dispute Resolution*, *Revise SQE: Tort Law* and *Revise SQE: Contract Law*.

Let's now consider the structure in question 1.

Assessment technique

Question 1 asks you to amend a precedent, which already gives the outline of a structure. The parts where you particularly need to draft are set out in four boxes. These boxes have been purposefully structured, so when drafting you should keep that structure in mind and not include irrelevant content.

1. Facts of the misconduct

This initial box is asking you to confirm the facts of the misconduct which satisfies s 101. You might have noted that there are five different misconduct gateways which could be the basis of your application to admit bad character. For a detailed explanation of those gateways, please see pages 127–8. If the misconduct is a previous conviction which is relevant to an important matter in issue between that defendant and the prosecution, you will need to explain whether you rely on (a) the fact of that conviction, or (b) the circumstances of that offence. If (b), you will need to set out the facts on which you rely.

2. How you will prove those facts, if in dispute

In other words, what evidence are you going to produce to the court? Remember that the burden of proof is on the prosecution, who must provide evidence that a defendant should have their bad character admitted into proceedings.

3. Reasons why the evidence is admissible

In essence you are concluding why the evidence discussed in point 2 is admissible by linking back to the gateway or gateways of s 101 of the Criminal Justice Act 2003, on which you are seeking to rely.

4. Reasons for any extension of time required

This box should only be completed if the notice is served late. As per Rule 21.4(3) of the Criminal Procedure Rules, the prosecutor must serve any such notice more than 20 business days after the defendant pleads not guilty in a magistrates' court; or ten business days after the defendant pleads not guilty in the Crown Court. An explanation as to why the notice is late is required before the decision is made by the court to admit the evidence.

HAVE A GO

Follow this structure:
- Start by outlining the facts.
- Then explain what evidence proves those facts.
- Conclude by linking to the legal principle.

This is comparable to structures you might remember from undergraduate study, such as:
- IRAC (issue, rule, application, conclusion)
- STAR (situation, task, actions, result)
- CARR (context, action, result, reflection).

Try to stay within the parameters of the four headings given in Attachment 3, and avoid discussing irrelevant content in the wrong box.

STEP 3 ENSURE THE WRITING STYLE AND LANGUAGE ARE APPROPRIATE FOR THE DRAFTED DOCUMENT

As already mentioned, to be competent by the SRA's standard your legal drafting must be clear, precise, concise and include acceptable language. For a reminder of what clear, precise, concise and acceptable language means, please see page 5.

Using appropriate language is very important when drafting a legal document. The documents need to be precise and avoid any ambiguity that may impact your client's position.

HAVE A GO

Practise writing in a style which is appropriate for a court application. The contents should be concise, precise and persuasive.

When drafting you should use an active tense, in the present tense rather than future. For an explanation of the difference between active and passive tense, see Chapter 3, page 101.

Assessment technique

Make sure you know the difference between past, present and future tenses.
- The past tense discusses actions completed in the past. For example:
  'The defendant was convicted of criminal damage.'
- The present tense describes actions happening in the present. For example:
  'The defendant is being convicted of criminal damage.'
- The future tense describes actions which will be completed at a later stage. For example:
  'The defendant will be convicted of criminal damage.'

Your use of tenses will significantly affect the meaning of the document, which is why it is very important to use the appropriate tense when drafting.

■ YOUR TURN

Have a go now at drafting a notice to introduce evidence of a defendant's bad character based on question 1.
- Remember the stepped approach on pages 125–30.
- Make sure you refer to the SRA's assessment criteria on page 119.
- Timings are important: you will have 45 minutes in the assessment to prepare and write your answer. Use this as an opportunity to practise your time management skills by timing yourself.

EVALUATING YOUR ANSWER

Once you have attempted to draft the notice, mark it yourself against the SQE2 legal drafting assessment criteria. Do you think your attempt met the threshold?

Now compare your attempt with the 'Key legal points' box and two sample answers below. A circled number indicates that commentary is provided for this part of the answer. The commentary will explain whether or not the sample answer is likely to meet the SQE2 standard threshold.

➡Key legal points: question 1

The defence is able to argue for the exclusion of the defendant's bad character under s 101(3) of the Criminal Justice Act 2003. Section 101(3) prevents a court from admitting evidence under subsections (d) and (g) if the admission of that evidence would have such an adverse effect on the fairness of the proceedings that the court ought not to admit it.

Under Criminal Procedure Rule 21.4(5), a party who objects to the introduction of the evidence identified by such a notice must apply to the court to determine the objection, then serve an application on the court officer, and each other party not more than ten business days after service of the notice. Under section (c), the application should explain:

    (i)   which, if any, facts of the misconduct set out in the notice that party disputes,

    (ii) what, if any, facts of the misconduct that party admits instead,

    (iii) why the evidence is not admissible,

    (iv) why it would be unfair to admit the evidence, and

    (v) any other objection to the notice.

■ SAMPLE ANSWER 1 TO QUESTION 1

NOTICE TO INTRODUCE EVIDENCE OF A DEFENDANT'S BAD CHARACTER
(Criminal Procedure Rules, rule 21.4(2))

Case details
Name of defendant: *Lynne Parsons*
Court: *Magistrates' Court*
Case reference number: *MG03064*
Charge(s): *Inflicting criminal damage contrary to sections 1(1) and 4 of the Criminal Damage Act 1971 on 10 January 202#.*

This notice is given by the prosecutor.

I want to introduce evidence of the bad character of Lynne Parsons on the following ground(s) in the Criminal Justice Act 2003:

☐ **it is important explanatory evidence: s.101(1)(c).**

☑ **it is relevant to an important matter in issue between that defendant and the prosecution: s.101(1)(d).** ❶

☐ **it has substantial probative value in relation to an important matter in issue between that defendant and a co-defendant: s.101(1)(e).**

☐ **it is evidence to correct a false impression given by that defendant: s.101(1)(f).**

☑ **that defendant has made an attack on another person's character: s.101(1)(g).** ❷

<u>How to use this form</u>
1. **Complete the boxes above and give the details required in the boxes below.**
   If you use an electronic version of this form, the boxes will expand. If you use a paper version and need more space, you may attach extra sheets.
2. **Sign and date the completed form.**
3. **Send a copy of the completed form to:**
   (a) the court, and
   (b) each other party to the case.

<u>Notes:</u>
1. You must send this form so as to reach the recipients within the time prescribed by Criminal Procedure Rule 21.4(3) or (4). The court may extend that time limit, **but if you are late you must explain why.**

2. A party who objects to the introduction of the evidence must apply to the court under Criminal Procedure Rule 21.4(5) **not more than 14 days after service of this notice.**

---

1) **Facts of the misconduct.** If the misconduct is a previous conviction, explain whether you rely on (a) the fact of that conviction, or (b) the circumstances of that offence. If (b), set out the facts on which you rely.

   The defendant was convicted of criminal damage in May 2023 and criminal damage in November 2023. The fact of these offences will be relied on to establish her propensity to commit offences of the type charged.

   The defendant has made an attack on the character of the prosecutions witness, Leah Flossie. The defendant attacked the character of the prosecution witness during a police interview on 20 January 202# when she called the prosecution witness a liar. ❸

---

2) **How you will prove those facts, if in dispute.** A party who objects to the introduction of the evidence must explain which, if any, of the facts set out above are in dispute. Explain in outline on what you will then rely to prove those facts, eg whether you rely on (a) a certificate of conviction, (b) another official record (and if so, which), or (c) other evidence (and if so, what).

   Evidence of the defendant's certificates of previous convictions will be produced. Evidence of the defendant's police interview transcript will be produced. The officer in the case will be called to adduce this evidence. ❹

---

3) **Reasons why the evidence is admissible.** Explain why the evidence is admissible, by reference to the provision(s) of the Criminal Justice Act 2003 on which you rely.

   Section 101(1)(d) Criminal Justice Act 2003 – relevant to an important matter in issue between the prosecution and the defence.

   Convictions recorded for criminal damage in May 2023, assault ABH in August 2023 and criminal damage in November 2023 establishing the defendant's propensity to commit offences of the type charged.

   The conviction for criminal damage in November 2023 establishes a propensity to be untruthful, having pleaded not guilty.

   Section 101(1)(g) Criminal Justice Act 2003 – that the defendant has made an attack on another person's character. ❺

4) **Reasons for any extension of time required.** If this notice is served late, explain why.

   N/A ❻

Signed:..
[prosecutor]

Date:................................

COMMENTARY

1 The prosecution can apply under s 101(1)(d) of the Criminal Justice Act 2003 on the basis that the bad character is relevant to an important matter in issue between the defendant and the prosecution. Section 103 of the Criminal Justice Act 2003 states that the 'matter' in issue includes whether the defendant has a propensity to commit offences of the kind with which they are charged. The candidate has correctly identified from the memorandum of convictions that the defendant has two recent previous convictions for criminal damage, which is arguably demonstrating propensity as per *R v Hanson* [2005].

2 The candidate has rightly also applied under s 101(1)(g) of the Criminal Justice Act 2003. This is because the defendant has attacked the prosecution witness when questioned under caution, which per s 106(1)(c) of the Criminal Justice Act 2003 is deemed evidence of an imputation. In the police interview transcript (Attachment 2), the defendant states: 'I know it was Leah Flossie who has told you it was me. She is a liar. She has had it in for me ever since I slept with her boyfriend.' This would amount to an attack on Leah Flossie's character. Where the court determines that an attack has taken place, the defendant's bad character becomes admissible. The candidate has therefore demonstrated that they are able to comprehensively apply the law to the evidence provided.

3 The facts of the misconduct are correctly provided in this part of the document. The candidate is seeking to introduce bad character based on two grounds: (1) it is relevant to an important matter in issue between that defendant and the prosecution on the basis that there are relevant previous convictions, and (2) the defendant has made an attack on the character of a prosecution witness, Leah Flossie. For the first point, the candidate has correctly noted that there is more than one previous conviction, which demonstrates a propensity to commit offences of the same nature as per *R v Hanson* [2005].

4 This section of the precedent requires details of how you will prove the facts listed in the first box and what evidence you will rely on. The candidate has correctly identified that Attachments 1 and 2 in the question should be submitted as evidence. In this case a certificate of conviction, another official record namely the interview transcript and the officer in the case, will be used to evidence the facts. If a party objects to the introduction of the evidence, they must explain which, if any, of the facts set out are in dispute and so it is very important for the candidate to use precise wording to accurately describe the evidence that will be relied on.

5 This section requires an explanation of the evidence and why it should be admitted. The candidate has extracted the correct details from Attachments 1 and 2 and also quoted the correct legislation, to present a strong case that the defendant has a propensity to commit offences of the same type as the one she is currently charged with.

6 This section is not applicable, which is why N/A has been written. It is important not to include information that is incorrect or irrelevant.

Does this answer meet the threshold?

The sample answer uses clear and precise language which is in the correct tense. The words and phrases are suitably formal for the document being drafted and the correct legal terminology is used. The answer is concise, using as few words as possible without compromising the quality of the answer.

The answer is structured appropriately and logically. The flow and direction of each paragraph is clear. The document is legally correct and comprehensive, which means that the drafting is legally effective and sufficiently detailed in the context of the situation; for example, the correct case details are included at the top of the document. There are no professional conduct issues arising from the drafting of the notice.

On balance, this answer is likely to meet the SQE2 assessment criteria.

Now let's consider the second sample answer to question 1.

■ SAMPLE ANSWER 2 TO QUESTION 1

NOTICE TO INTRODUCE EVIDENCE OF A DEFENDANT'S
BAD CHARACTER
(Criminal Procedure Rules, rule 21.4(2))

Case details
Name of defendant: *Leah Flossie* ❶
Court: *Magistrates' Court*
Case reference number: *MG03064*
Charge(s): *Inflicting criminal damage contrary to sections 1(1) and 4 of the Criminal Damage Act 1971 on 10 January 202#.*

This notice is given by [the prosecutor]

I want to introduce evidence of the bad character of Lynne Parsons on the following ground(s) in the Criminal Justice Act 2003:
- ☑ **it is important explanatory evidence: s.101(1)(c).** ❷
- ☐ **it is relevant to an important matter in issue between that defendant and the prosecution: s.101(1)(d).**
- ☑ **it has substantial probative value in relation to an important matter in issue between that defendant and a co-defendant: s.101(1)(e).** ❸
- ☐ **it is evidence to correct a false impression given by that defendant: s.101(1)(f).**
- ☐ **that defendant has made an attack on another person's character: s.101(1)(g).**

How to use this form
1. **Complete the boxes above and give the details required in the boxes below.** If you use an electronic version of this form, the boxes will expand. If you use a paper version and need more space, you may attach extra sheets.
2. **Sign and date the completed form.**
3. **Send a copy of the completed form to:**
   (a) the court, and
   (b) each other party to the case.

Notes:
1. You must send this form so as to reach the recipients within the time prescribed by Criminal Procedure Rule 21.4(3) or (4). The court may extend that time limit, **but if you are late you must explain why.**

2. A party who objects to the introduction of the evidence must apply to the court under Criminal Procedure Rule 21.4(5) **not more than 14 days after service of this notice.**

---

1) **Facts of the misconduct.** If the misconduct is a previous conviction, explain whether you rely on (a) the fact of that conviction, or (b) the circumstances of that offence. If (b), set out the facts on which you rely.

The defendant was convicted of criminal damage in May 2023, assault ABH in August 2023 and criminal damage in November 2023. The defendant was intoxicated when committing all of these offences. This is important explanatory evidence because the defendant was also drunk when committing this offence.

The defendant was convicted of criminal damage in November 2023 following a not guilty plea. The fact of the conviction will be relied on to establish her propensity to be untruthful.

The identification of the defendant has substantial probative value in relation to an important matter in issue between that defendant and a co-defendant. ❹

---

2) **How you will prove those facts, if in dispute.** A party who objects to the introduction of the evidence must explain which, if any, of the facts set out above are in dispute. Explain in outline on what you will then rely to prove those facts, eg whether you rely on (a) a certificate of conviction, (b) another official record (and if so, which), or (c) other evidence (and if so, what).

Evidence of the defendant's certificates of previous convictions will be produced. Evidence of the defendant's alcohol abuse will be produced. ❺

---

3) **Reasons why the evidence is admissible.** Explain why the evidence is admissible, by reference to the provision(s) of the Criminal Justice Act 2003 on which you rely.

Section 101(1)(c) Criminal Justice Act 2003 – it is important explanatory evidence.

Convictions recorded for criminal damage in May 2023, assault ABH in August 2023 and criminal damage in November 2023 establishing the defendant's propensity to commit offences of violence.

The conviction for criminal damage in November 2023 establishes a propensity to be untruthful having pleaded not guilty.

Section 101(1)(e) Criminal Justice Act 2003 – it has substantial probative value in relation to an important matter in issue between that defendant and a co-defendant. ❻

---

4) **Reasons for any extension of time required.** If this notice is served late, explain why.

An extension of time is required. The court and defendant were put on notice at the hearing on the 15 February that the prosecution sought to admit evidence of the defendant's bad character into trial. ❼

Signed: . . . .
[prosecutor]

Date: . . . .

COMMENTARY

❶ The defendant's name has been entered here as Leah Flossie. This is clearly an error, as this is the prosecution witness's name. Although this might be a simple mistake, it would have substantial ramification in the case if it was not corrected. The candidate has failed to apply the law correctly at the first opportunity.

❷ The candidate should have removed the square brackets around 'the prosecutor'. Section 101(1)(c) does not apply on the facts of this scenario. Put simply, the court does not need to know about the previous convictions to understand the evidence in the current case. The candidate should have applied under s 101(1)(d) of the Criminal

Justice Act 2003, on the basis that the bad character is relevant to an important matter in issue between the defendant and the prosecution.

3 Section 101(1)(e) also does not apply on these facts. This gateway can sometimes be confused with s 101(1)(d), but s 101(1)(e) specifically relates to co-defendants. We know from the information that there are no co-defendants in this matter. The candidate should have applied under s 101(1)(g) of the Criminal Justice Act 2003, on the basis that the defendant has already attacked the prosecution witness when questioned under caution (s 106(1)(c) of the Criminal Justice Act 2003).

4 This section should contain the facts of the misconduct, but the candidate has not included correct information. Whilst the offences listed in the first sentence are accurate, it is not correct to say (in the second sentence) that the defendant was intoxicated when committing all the offences. From the information given, the candidate cannot make that assertion. To include this would breach paragraph 1.4 of the Code of Conduct for Solicitors. Furthermore, the third sentence states that intoxication is important explanatory evidence. This is incorrect. Important explanatory evidence means that you need to know about the defendant's previous convictions to understand the evidence in the case, which is not relevant here.

Code of Conduct for Solicitors, RELs and RFLs link

Rule 1.4 states that you must not mislead or attempt to mislead your clients, the court or others, either by your own actions or omissions, or being complicit in the acts or omissions of others (including your client). This is an important rule to bear in mind: in the context of sample answer 2 for question 1, if the answer is sent to court as written, the solicitor will have breached the Code of Conduct and could face serious implications including a fine and/or their practising certificate revoked.

The second paragraph discusses a propensity to be untruthful. However, the conviction does not establish untruthfulness or a propensity to be untruthful. This is therefore legally incorrect.

The third paragraph discusses identification being an issue in this case, which is incorrect and misleading. It also suggests that there is a co-defendant, when there is not. This level of inaccuracy will have significant implications as it could be suggested that the candidate is breaching the SRA Code of Conduct for Solicitors, RELs and RFLs by misleading the court (1.4).

5 The candidate has correctly stated that certificates of previous convictions will be produced, but evidence of the defendant's alcohol abuse is not relevant.

6 This section does not provide the reasons for the evidence to be admissible, and instead just reiterates the legislation grounds. The second paragraph mentions offences of violence, but this does not establish the defendant's propensity to commit offences of the type that has been charged. Moreover, that issue is not relevant to s 101(1)(c). Finally, as noted under point 4, untruthfulness should not be discussed, as it is not relevant.

7 This section is technically incorrect and should have not been completed as the notice is being served in time. When considering whether an extension should be granted, the court would need: (1) to consider the reason for the failure to comply. The court would ordinarily wish to know when the relevant inquiries had been initiated and in broad terms why they had not been completed within the time allowed; (2) to be satisfied that there is no conceivable prejudice to the defendant, bearing in mind that she would be aware of the facts of her earlier convictions. Had the application been out of time, the paragraph should have included:

- why there is a failure to comply with the timescales; and
- that the court and defence were put on notice about the intention for an application to be made.

Does this answer meet the threshold?

The answer is legally incorrect throughout: the incorrect grounds have been highlighted and false information has been given to the court. Rather than resolve ethical and professional conduct issues, the document has created new ones, as the information contained is misleading for the court and thus breaches paragraph 1.4 of the Code of Conduct for Solicitors. Structurally, the necessary information has not been provided in the right places, which impacts the overall flow of the notice. On balance, this answer is not competent and would not meet the threshold standard for SQE2.

The SRA can assess any of the areas on the SQE2 specification. Below is another example of how a different part of the specification, business organisations, rules and procedures, could arise in the context of SQE2 legal drafting.

■ QUESTION 2

Email to candidate

From: Partner
Sent: 15 September 202#
To: Candidate
Subject: Partnership agreement

I have had a meeting last week with four new clients who are instructing us to assist with the creation of a partnership. The partners are Sabine Gubta, Andrew Donald, David Rednall and Da-Xia Chen. They explained that they are all to have equal status within the partnership, they will enjoy equal management responsibilities and will contribute equal capital funding. They have not yet assigned roles to each other.

We discussed the general contents that should be included in a partnership agreement, and I subsequently drafted an agreement.

During our meeting, the partners requested I leave drafting clauses regarding Admission of a new Partner, Retirement, Expulsion and Provisions relating to death, retirement, deemed retirement or expulsion until a later date, because they had not yet agreed those terms.

I have now received an email from David Rednall (Attachment 1). It seems they have now been able to agree on what the expulsion clause should include.

Please draft the expulsion clause using the precedent provided (Attachment 2). Please carefully consider the email provided in Attachment 1, and draft as per the client's instructions. The clause should be number 16 in the agreement.

Thanks

Partner

Attachments:

Email from David Rednall
Partnership Agreement Precedent

Note to candidates:

The board minutes that are referred to in Attachment 1 have not been produced in consideration of the time constraints of this assessment.

Attachment 1

Email from David Rednall

From: David Rednall
Sent: 14 September 202#
To: Partner
Subject: Partnership Agreement
Attachments: Board Minutes.PDF

Dear Partner

Following the meeting last week, we have all discussed the other clauses that need to be added to the agreement. We have managed to agree what should be included in the expulsion clause.

Please can your draft document state that we can expel the relevant partner by notice in writing in the following circumstances:

a   The Partner fails to pay any money owed to the Partnership within 14 days of being asked in writing;
b   The Partner suffers from a mental disorder which prevents them from performing their duties;
c   The Partner is ill for a period of eight months, and this prevents them from performing their duties;
d   The Partner engages in conduct which will have an adverse impact on the business or will breach the Partnership Agreement; or
e   The Partner has had a permanent injury for the preceding six months which prevents them from performing their duties.

We also think it would also be useful to include something about what should happen if one of us ceases to hold the authorisation required for the normal performance of our duties as a partner. In this circumstance, we think that the other partners should be able to expel the relevant partner by notice in writing immediately upon the ruling or decision in question takes effect.

I have attached the board minutes which confirm the contents of this email and that I am able to give these instructions on behalf of the company.

Looking forward to receiving a draft once you have done this.

Yours sincerely

David Rednall

Attachments:

Board Minutes

Attachment 2

Partnership Agreement Precedent template

Expulsion
1.1   A Partner may be expelled if they:
    1.1.1   commit a serious breach or repeated breaches of this agreement;
    1.1.2   engage in conduct that may seriously harm the Business;
    1.1.3   have been unable to perform their duties due to illness, injury, or other reasons for a continuous period of at least [six OR 12] months immediately preceding the date the notice referred to in this clause [ ] was served or a cumulative period of at least [six OR 12] months within the 24-month period preceding the date the notice referred to in this clause [ ] was served;
    1.1.4   become a patient under section 145(1) of the Mental Health Act 1983 or any successor legislation;
    1.1.5   no longer have any required qualification, certification, or authorisation needed for the day-to-day performance of their duties as a Partner;
    1.1.6   fail to pay any amounts owed to the Partnership within 28 days of a written request from the Management Committee;
    1.1.7   have a bankruptcy order made against them; or
    1.1.8   have their share in the Partnership subjected to a charging order under the Partnership Act 1890.

1.2   Expulsion Process
    1.2.1   The Management Committee may expel the relevant Partner by written notice, provided there is consent from a special resolution.

1.3   Expulsion for Loss of Professional Qualification
    1.3.1   If a Partner faces proceedings that may lead to the loss of a professional qualification, certification or authorisation necessary for their role, and the loss may result in the dissolution of the Partnership under section 34 of the Partnership Act 1890, the Partners may agree, by special resolution, to expel that Partner. Written notice of expulsion can be given in advance, and it will take effect immediately before the relevant ruling or decision takes effect.

*   *   *

■ YOUR TURN

Have a go at drafting this clause for the partnership agreement as required in question 2.
- Remember the stepped approach on pages 125–30.
- Make sure you refer to the SRA's assessment criteria on page 119.
- Timings are important: you will have 45 minutes in the assessment to prepare and write your answer. Use this as an opportunity to practise your time management skills by timing yourself.

SQE 1 Functioning legal knowledge link

If you need to revise your FLK of this area of law, see chapter 2 of ***Revise SQE: Business Law and Practice*** which provides an overview of partnerships under the Partnership Act 1890.

EVALUATING YOUR ANSWER

Once you have attempted to draft this clause, mark it yourself against the SQE2 legal drafting assessment criteria. Do you think your attempt met the threshold?

Now compare your attempt with the 'Key legal points' box and two sample answers below. A circled number indicates that commentary is provided for this part of the answer. The commentary will explain whether or not the sample answer is likely to meet the SQE2 standard threshold.

Code of Conduct for Solicitors, RELs and RFLs link

In question 2 you are instructed to act on behalf of a partnership. This means that you are representing the partnership and not individual partners. In the email setting out the instructions to candidate, it is explained that the partners all have equal status within the partnership, they will enjoy equal management responsibilities and will contribute equal capital funding. Their roles are yet to be assigned. This could be problematic for the solicitor. It is not clear which partner has the authority to confirm instructions to the solicitor on behalf of the partnership.

When instructed by a partnership or company, the solicitor must know who has authority to give instructions on behalf of the partnership and have some form of evidence that proves the authority of that person. This could be, for example, the board minutes, Power of Attorney or the constitutional documents of the company, eg memorandum and articles of association. This is because under paragraph 3.1 of the Code of Conduct, a solicitor can only act for clients on instructions from the client, or from someone properly authorised to provide instructions on their behalf.

➡ Key legal points: question 2

Under s 25 of the Partnership Act 1890, partners cannot expel a partner (even if most of the partners wish to do so) unless such a power has been conferred by the express agreement of the partners. That is why it is crucial that an expulsion clause is included in the partnership agreement.

The precedent above enables the partners to agree to expel a partner by special resolution, on certain specified grounds.

■ SAMPLE ANSWER 1 TO QUESTION 2

16 Expulsion ❶
16.1 A Partner may be expelled if they:
    16.1.1 commit a serious breach or repeated breaches of this agreement;
    16.1.2 engage in conduct that may seriously harm the Business; ❷
    16.1.3 have been unable to perform their duties due to illness, ~~injury, or other~~ reasons for a continuous period of at least *eight* months immediately preceding the date the notice referred to in this clause *16.1* was served or a cumulative period of at least *eight* months within the 24-month period preceding the date the notice referred to in this clause *16.1* was served;
    16.1.4 have been unable to perform their duties due to *permanent* injury, ~~illness or other reasons~~ for a continuous period of at least *six* months immediately preceding the date the notice referred to in this clause *16.1* was served

or a cumulative period of at least *six* months within the 24-month period preceding the date the notice referred to in this clause *16.1* was served; ❸

16.1.5 *suffer from a mental disorder*, become a patient under section 145(1) of the Mental Health Act 1983 or any successor legislation *which renders them unable to perform their duties as a Partner*; ❹

16.1.6 no longer have any required qualification, certification, or authorisation needed for the day-to-day performance of their duties as a Partner; ❺

16.1.7 fail to pay any amounts owed to the Partnership within 28*14* days of a written request from the Management Committee; ❻

16.1.8 have a bankruptcy order made against them; or ❼

16.1.9 have their share in the Partnership subjected to a charging order under the Partnership Act 1890. ❽

16.2 Expulsion Process

16.2.1 The Management Committee may expel the relevant Partner by written notice, provided there is consent from a special resolution.

16.3 Expulsion for Loss of Professional Qualification

16.3.1 If a Partner faces proceedings that may lead to the loss of a professional qualification, certification, or authorisation necessary for their role, and the loss may result in the dissolution of the Partnership under section 34 of the Partnership Act 1890, the Partners may agree, by special resolution, to expel that Partner. Written notice of expulsion can be given in advance, and it will take effect immediately before the relevant ruling or decision takes effect. ❾

COMMENTARY

❶ The clause has correctly been numbered as clause 16, which is in accordance with the instructions. This assists when structuring the whole document logically and appropriately. This heading also serves as an appropriate signpost to guide the reader through the partnership agreement.

❷ This has been specifically mentioned in the client's instructions and therefore must be included in the clause.

❸ The candidate has separated illness and injury, unlike in the original precedent. This correctly reflects the client's instruction that the time period should be different for illness and permanent injury. Because this paragraph has been added, the clause numbers have been amended throughout clause 16 (ie 1.1.4 on the precedent is now 16.1.5). The candidate could have considered adding 'permanent injury' as a defined term.

❹ Section 145(1) of the Mental Health Act 1983 defines mental disorder as the meaning given in s 1 (subject to s 86(4)). Within s 1, 'mental disorder' means any disorder or disability of the mind; and 'mentally disordered' shall be construed accordingly.

Note that clauses 16.1.3, 16.1.4 and 16.1.5 detail what will happen in the event a partner becomes incapacitated, whereas the clauses that follow focus on culpability. This is relevant when considering the structure of the clause. Whilst it may be tempting to follow the order of the instructions, ie starting with what should happen if the Partner fails to pay any money owed to the Partnership, try to stick to a logical order as the candidate has done here.

❺ Any 'qualification and certification' has been removed from this clause as per the clients' instructions. For further explanation regarding this clause see point 9 below.

❻ As per the client's instructions, 28 days has been correctly changed to 14 days.

❼ Whilst the clients have not specifically requested that this clause be included, the bankruptcy of a partner leads to automatic dissolution of the partnership under s 33(1) of the Partnership Act 1890, unless otherwise agreed. The clients' instructions do not specify that a different agreement has been reached, therefore it seems sensible for this clause to be included. The candidate would need to discuss this clause further with the clients; however, this is an attempt to draft a legally comprehensive clause which is in the clients' best interests as per SRA Principle 7.

8 Again this clause has not been specifically requested by the clients, but s 33(2) of the Partnership Act 1890 provides that where a partner allows their share in the partnership to be subjected to a charging order, the partnership may be dissolved at the request of the other partners. Whilst this option remains available to the other partners, clause 16.1.8 enables the affected partners to be expelled without a general dissolution. As with point 7, the candidate would need to discuss this clause with the client, but is attempting to draft a legally comprehensive clause in the clients' best interests as per SRA Principle 7.

9 This clause and clause 16.1.6 have been amended so that a partner is only required to cease to hold authorisation necessary for the normal performance of their duties to be expelled as per the instructions. Clause 16.2 is an attempt to get around s 34 of the Partnership Act 1890. Section 34 outlines the automatic provision for dissolution of a partnership where it becomes unlawful for a partnership to continue carrying on a business because a partner fails to maintain a qualification that they are required to hold to carry on that business.

Does this answer meet the threshold?

The clause uses clear, precise, concise and acceptable language. As discussed in point 3 of the commentary, the answer has been structured logically by putting all incapacity clauses together first and culpability clauses thereafter. The clauses have also been numbered correctly. The answer is drafted in such a way that it is legally correct, and the inclusion of further clauses outside the client's instructions demonstrates an understanding of the Partnership Act 1890 and an ability to exercise judgement to act in the clients' best interests as per SRA Principle 7.

On balance, it is likely that this answer meets the SRA threshold and would be deemed as competent.

Now let's consider the second sample answer to question 2.

■ SAMPLE ANSWER 2 TO QUESTION 2

1   Expulsion **1**
1.1   A **Parter** may be expelled if they:
    1.1.1 fail to pay any amounts owed to the Partnership within 28 days of a written request from the Management Committee;
    1.1.2 become a patient under section 145(1) of the Mental Health Act 1983 or any successor legislation;
    1.1.3 commit a serious breach or repeated breaches of this agreement;
    1.1.4 have been unable to perform their duties **as a Colleague** due to illness, injury, or other reasons for a continuous period of at least **sixt** months immediately preceding the date the notice referred to in this clause [-] was served or a cumulative period of at least **six** months within the 24-month period preceding the date the notice referred to in this clause [-] was served;
    1.1.5 no longer have any required qualification, certification, or authorisation needed for the day-to-day performance of their duties as a Partner;
    1.1.6 commit a serious breach or repeated breaches of this agreement;
    1.1.7 have a bankruptcy order made against them; or

~~1.1.8 have their share in the Partnership subjected to a charging order under the~~
~~Partnership Act 1890~~ **2**

1.2 Expulsion Process
    1.2.1 The Management Committee may expel the relevant Partner by written
    notice, provided there is consent from a special resolution.

1.3 Expulsion for Loss of Professional Qualification
    1.3.1 If a Partner faces proceedings that may lead to the loss of a professional
    qualification, certification, or authorisation necessary for their role, and the
    loss may result in the dissolution of the Partnership under section 34 of the
    Partnership Act 1890, the Partners may agree, by special resolution, to expel
    that Partner. Written notice of expulsion can be given in advance, and it will
    take effect immediately before the relevant ruling or decision takes effect. **3**

COMMENTARY

1 The clause has not been numbered correctly as per the instructions. There are also problems with the numbering throughout the document. This would present a wider structural issue for when the clause is added to the partnership agreement.

2 All of the clauses within 1.1 contain inaccuracies so that they do not reflect the clients' instructions. 'Six' and 'partner' are spelt incorrectly. Whilst misspelling 'partner' is less significant, inserting 'sixt' could affect the validity of the document as it could be misinterpreted to mean sixty rather than six.

Further inaccuracies include the following:
- Clause 1.1.1 has not been amended, which means that the time frame is incorrect.
- Clause 1.1.2 does not include the correct information as per the clients' instructions.
- Clause 1.1.3 has been removed and then added at clause 1.1.6. It is unclear why the candidate has done this, although it is appropriate that it remains included.
- Clause 1.1.4 makes no attempt to differentiate between illness and injury, so that the time frame for injury is incorrect. There is also no mention of permanent injury
- There has been no consideration of the Partnership Act's provisions.
- The terminology is inconsistent, referring to the Partners as a 'Partner' and then 'Colleague'. This is confusing and arguably a misrepresentation of what is meant.

See Chapter 1, page 5 for guidelines on how errors of spelling and grammar can affect your assessment.

3 This clause has not been amended at all and still contains qualifications and certification, which is not in accordance with the clients' instructions. This could pose a wider issue as it contravenes SRA Principle 2 for solicitors to act in a way that upholds public trust and confidence in their profession.

Does this answer meet the threshold?

The structure of this answer is not logical, and has followed the clients' list of requirements rather than adopting the structure provided in the precedent. The answer contains errors that affect the clarity and precision of the drafting. The drafted document lacks legal accuracy as it does not appear to consider what clauses should be incorporated as per the Partnership Act 1890.

The answer is not legally comprehensive and the candidate has not identified any ethical and professional conduct issues or attempted to resolve them honestly and with integrity. There has been no consideration of acting in the clients' best interests as per SRA Principle 7, and the candidate seems to have simply inserted the contents of the question and attachment into the document without interpreting it.

■ KEY POINT CHECKLIST

This chapter has covered the following key points:
- The SQE2 assessment criteria for legal drafting and how to apply them in the context of drafting first a notice to introduce evidence of a defendant's bad character, and then a clause for a partnership agreement.
- Advice on how to structure your response in an SQE2 legal drafting assessment.
- Sample answers that show what is either likely or unlikely to meet the SRA's Day One Solicitor competency.

■ SUMMARY AND REFLECTION

To succeed in the SQE2 legal drafting assessment, ensure that you read all the information before beginning to write your answer. Your document must be thorough and cover all essential details so that it addresses the necessary legal requirements and complies with relevant laws, regulations and legal standards.

Make sure your language is clear and precise and avoids ambiguity. The document you are drafting should be understood by all parties, so be consistent in your terminology and definitions to avoid any confusion or misinterpretation.

Keep checking that you are tailoring the document to the specific needs and circumstances of the parties involved, rather than relying solely on generic templates.

Finally, try to review your work before the end of the assessment, to catch any errors/ omissions and refine the document for accuracy and comprehensiveness.

Final words

We hope that the guidance and examples contained in this book have helped to put into context how to use your practice skills to ensure you reach the SQE2 grading criteria. Remember, above all, this is an assessment and the examiner needs to see evidence that you have met the criteria in order for you to pass the threshold. Always keep this in the back of your mind when taking your SQE2 assessments.

While this book is designed to aid your learning and provide helpful tips on how to pass your SQE2 assessments, it is no substitute for practice. All skills are improved with repetition and refining your technique, and legal skills are no exception to this rule. Take any opportunity you can to write letters, draft legal documents and practise your interviewing and advocacy skills. Reflect carefully on your performance after each exercise:
- What could you have done better?
- Did you meet all of the grading criteria applicable to that particular skill?
- Do you need to fill any gaps in your legal knowledge?

Constant practice and self-reflection are the keys to success.

Finally, the team at *Revise SQE* wish you the best of luck in your SQE2 assessments!

Appendix

PERFORMANCE INDICATORS FOR SQE2
CASE AND MATTER ANALYSIS ASSESSMENT CRITERIA

Skills	Indicators demonstrating competence	Indicators that do not demonstrate competence
Identify relevant facts	• The candidate selects facts that are important in ensuring the client's needs/objectives are met, or are relevant to the legal analysis, from the documentation provided	• The candidate refers to all facts from the documentation, regardless of whether or not they are important in meeting the client's objectives or relevant to their legal analysis • The candidate refers only to irrelevant facts • The candidate does not refer to sufficient relevant facts to support the legal analysis
Provide client-focused advice (ie advice that demonstrates an understanding of the problem from the client's point of view and what the client wants to achieve, not just from a legal perspective)	• The candidate demonstrates an understanding of the client's problem from the client's perspective • The candidate addresses the client's legal problem, any relevant commercial considerations and/or the client's personal circumstances, priorities, objectives and constraints	• The candidate does not approach or appreciate the client's problem from the client's perspective • The candidate does not focus on the issues identified by the client
Use clear, precise, concise and acceptable language	• The reader understands the candidate's use of language and clarity of expression • The candidate avoids unnecessary technical terms/legal jargon	• The reader struggles to understand the candidate's use of language; the answer lacks clarity and/or is poorly expressed • The reader's understanding is adversely affected by the density, length or brevity of the answer • The candidate uses unnecessary technical terms/legal jargon

Law	Indicators demonstrating competence	Indicators that do not demonstrate competence
Apply the law correctly to the client's situation	• The candidate identifies the relevant fundamental legal principles in accordance with the SQE2 assessment specification and applies them correctly to the facts of the client's case	• The candidate does not identify and correctly apply the relevant legal principles to the facts of the client's case • The candidate does not apply the relevant legal principles in a way that addresses the client's needs and concerns
Apply the law comprehensively to the client's situation, identifying any ethical and professional conduct issues and exercising judgement to resolve them honestly and with integrity	• The candidate's legal analysis is sufficiently detailed in the context of the client's case, eg assessing information to identify key issues and risks; reaching reasonable conclusions supported by relevant evidence • Where relevant, the candidate recognises ethical issues and exercises effective judgement in addressing them in accordance with the SRA Principles and rules of professional conduct	• The candidate's legal analysis is not sufficiently detailed in the context of the client's case, eg the candidate demonstrates little or no understanding of the key issues and risks; fails to apply the law to the facts to reach reasonable conclusions • The candidate does not recognise ethical issues or exercise effective judgement in addressing them in accordance with the SRA Principles and rules of professional conduct

PERFORMANCE INDICATORS FOR SQE2 LEGAL RESEARCH ASSESSMENT CRITERIA

Skills	*Indicators demonstrating competence*	*Indicators that do not demonstrate competence*
Identify and use relevant sources and information	• The candidate selects relevant information about the legal issue, or the client's problem, from the primary and/or secondary sources provided, eg o the candidate identifies relevant legislation/cases and/or legal explanations/ commentary in a practitioner's text, or legal encyclopaedia o the candidate extracts relevant material, such as particular provision(s) from a statute, or legal rule(s) from the Civil Procedure Rules • The candidate uses their findings to substantiate/ support their answer to the question(s) asked	• The candidate selects only irrelevant information from the primary and/or secondary sources provided • The candidate selects insufficient relevant information from the primary and/or secondary sources provided • The candidate is unable to distinguish between information that is relevant to the legal issue or the client's problem, and information that is irrelevant, eg the candidate's answer contains information drawn from all sources regardless of relevance, or from a number of irrelevant sources • The candidate does not use their findings to substantiate/ support the answer to the question(s) asked
Provide advice that is client-focused and addresses the client's problem	• The candidate demonstrates an understanding of the client's problem from the client's perspective, eg the candidate addresses the client's legal problem, any relevant commercial considerations and/or the client's priorities, objectives and constraints	• The candidate does not understand the problem from the client's perspective, eg they focus on irrelevant issues/provide advice that does not take into account the client's priorities, objectives or constraints, or is inappropriate for the client's situation
Use clear, precise, concise and acceptable language	• The candidate uses understandable and simple language to convey facts and information effectively • The candidate uses correct legal terminology where necessary	• The reader struggles to understand the candidate's use of language; the answer lacks clarity and/or is poorly expressed • The reader's understanding is adversely affected by the density or brevity of the answer • The candidate uses unnecessary or confusing technical terms/legal jargon

Law	Indicators demonstrating competence	Indicators that do not demonstrate competence
Apply the law correctly to the client's situation	• The candidate identifies the relevant legal principles and applies them correctly to the facts of the client's case	• The candidate does not identify and apply the correct legal principles to the facts of the client's case • The candidate identifies the correct legal principles but misapplies them to the client's case
Apply the law comprehensively to the client's situation, identifying any ethical and professional conduct issues and exercising judgement to resolve them honestly and with integrity	• The candidate's legal analysis is sufficiently detailed in the context of the facts of the case, eg the candidate draws on multiple sources of information to address the legal issue/client's problem effectively • Where relevant, the candidate recognises ethical issues and exercises effective judgement in addressing them in accordance with the SRA Principles and rules of professional conduct	• The candidate's legal analysis is not sufficiently detailed in the context of the facts of the client's case • The candidate does not recognise ethical issues or exercise effective judgement in addressing them in accordance with the SRA Principles and rules of professional conduct

PERFORMANCE INDICATORS FOR SQE2 LEGAL WRITING ASSESSMENT CRITERIA

Skills	Indicators demonstrating competence	Indicators that do not demonstrate competence
Include relevant facts	• The candidate refers to and/or addresses the salient facts provided in their instructions. Salient facts could include facts that are important in ensuring the client's needs/objectives are met, or relevant to legal advice	• The candidate includes many facts in their answer that have no bearing on their legal advice
Use a logical structure	• The candidate's presentation of information is well organised, set out clearly and easy to follow • The reader is able to understand the candidate's answer without difficulty	• The candidate's presentation of information is confused and rambling • The reader is unable to follow or understand the candidate's answer
Advice/content is client- and recipient-focused	• The candidate demonstrates an understanding of the client's circumstances including their needs, objectives and priorities • The candidate, where relevant and appropriate, explores options and advises on strategies and solutions • The candidate takes into account who the client is; recognises the key issues in the case and considers any risks • Where appropriate, the candidate imparts any difficult or unwelcome news clearly and sensitively	• The candidate does not understand the client's perspective, eg they focus on irrelevant issues/provide extraneous advice/fail to advise on relevant options, strategies and solutions • The candidate fails to take into account who the client is and does not recognise the key issues in the case or consider any risks • The candidate lacks empathy or sensitivity if imparting difficult or unwelcome news
Use clear, precise, concise and acceptable language that is appropriate to the recipient	• The reader understands the candidate's use of language and clarity of expression • The candidate's language is appropriate to the recipient and the situation • The candidate avoids unnecessary technical terms/legal jargon • The candidate uses formalities appropriate to the context and purpose of the communication	• The reader struggles to understand the candidate's use of language; the answer lacks clarity and/or is poorly expressed • The reader's understanding is adversely affected by the density or brevity of the answer • The candidate uses language that is not appropriate to the recipient and/or the situation, eg the candidate adopts an essay-style approach • The candidate uses unnecessary or confusing technical terms/legal jargon

Law	Indicators demonstrating competence	Indicators that do not demonstrate competence
Apply the law correctly to the client's situation	• The candidate identifies the correct legal principles and applies them correctly to the facts of the case	• The candidate does not identify the correct legal principles • The candidate does not apply the legal principles correctly to the client's situation
Apply the law comprehensively to the client's situation, identifying any ethical and professional conduct issues and exercising judgement to resolve them honestly and with integrity	• The candidate's writing is of sufficient detail in the context of the client's situation and the relevant factual and legal issues • Where relevant, the candidate recognises ethical issues and exercises effective judgement in addressing them in accordance with the SRA Principles and rules of professional conduct	• The candidate's writing is not sufficiently detailed in the context of the client's situation and the relevant factual and legal issues • The candidate does not recognise ethical issues or exercise effective judgement in addressing them in accordance with the SRA Principles and rules of professional conduct

PERFORMANCE INDICATORS FOR SQE2 LEGAL DRAFTING ASSESSMENT CRITERIA

Skills	Indicators demonstrating competence	Indicators that do not demonstrate competence
Use clear, precise, concise and acceptable language	• The candidate uses understandable and simple language to convey facts and information effectively • The candidate uses words and phrases that are suitably formal for the document being drafted • The candidate uses correct legal terminology where necessary • The document uses as few words as possible without compromising the quality of the answer	• The candidate's answer is consistently wordy, repetitive or confusing and cannot be easily understood • The meaning of the document cannot be ascertained because it contains few words • The candidate uses inappropriate language, eg the language is too informal or casual • The candidate uses unnecessary technical terms/ legal jargon throughout
Structure the document appropriately and logically	• The candidate presents facts and information in a methodical way, eg the focus, flow and direction of each paragraph is clear and appropriate signposts are used to guide the reader through the document • The way in which the candidate sets out the contents of the document achieve its purpose	• The candidate's arrangement of facts or information is disjointed or confusing, eg the paragraphing or sequencing of information is illogical • The way in which the candidate sets out the contents of the document does not achieve its purpose
Law	Indicators demonstrating competence	Indicators that do not demonstrate competence
Draft a document that is legally correct	• The candidate identifies the correct legal principles in accordance with the SQE2 assessment specification and applies them correctly in their drafting • The candidate's drafting is legally effective, eg the document contains all key information or the names of relevant parties	• The candidate does not identify the correct legal principles • The candidate does not apply the legal principles correctly in their drafting • The candidate's drafting is not legally effective
Draft a document that is legally comprehensive, identifying any ethical and professional conduct issues and exercising judgement to resolve them honestly and with integrity	• The candidate's drafting is sufficiently detailed in the context of the client's situation and the relevant factual and legal issues • Where relevant, the candidate recognises ethical issues and exercises effective judgement in addressing them in accordance with the SRA Principles and rules of professional conduct	• The candidate's drafting is not sufficiently detailed in the context of the client's situation and the relevant factual and legal issues • The candidate does not recognise ethical issues or exercise effective judgement in addressing them in accordance with the SRA Principles and rules of professional conduct